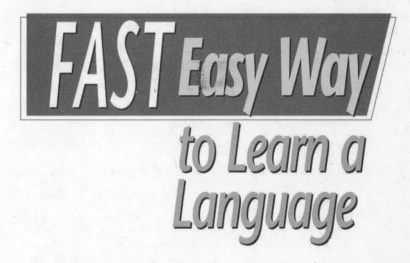

FAST Easy Way to Learn a Language

BILL HANDLEY

Wrightbooks

First published 2005 by Wrightbooks
an imprint of John Wiley & Sons Australia, Ltd
42 McDougall Street, Milton Qld 4064

Offices also in Sydney and Melbourne

Typeset in Bembo 11/15 pt

© Bill Handley 2005

National Library of Australia
Cataloguing-in-Publication data:

Handley, Bill.

Fast, easy way to learn a language.

Includes index.

ISBN 0 7314 0335 5.

1. Language acquisition. 2. Language and languages.
3. Second language acquisition. I. Title.

401.93

Cover design by Rob Cowpe

Printed in Australia by Griffin Press

10 9 8 7 6 5 4 3 2 1

The numbers given in the chapter headers throughout this book are written in the following languages: English, Greek, French, German, Spanish, Russian, Indonesian/Malay and Finnish.

Contents

Other books by Bill Handley

Teach Your Children Tables

Speed Mathematics: Secrets of Lightning Mental Calculation

Speed Maths for Kids: Helping Kids Achieve Their Full Potential

Preface

I have written this book because I love learning languages. I believe that anyone should be able to learn a language superbly well in a year. You should be speaking the language in your first week of study.

This book is about learning a language the fast, easy way. If you really need to, you should be able to learn almost any language quite well in a month. After just one month, you should be able to travel through the country, ask directions, drive, order meals, book a room and hold simple conversations. I tell in this book how I learnt basic Italian in two weeks without taking time off from my job or spending long hours studying, using a very good language course that taught me the language that I needed. It is possible to learn to speak intelligent and useful sentences in a week. I will show you how you can do it too.

Whatever your reason for learning a new language, whether you want to know enough to survive a weekend in the country or you want to be able to give presentations or negotiate in the language, this book can help you learn it faster and more easily.

Bill Handley
Melbourne, Australia
August 2005
bhandley@speedmathematics.com

Introduction

I was already fascinated by the idea of learning and speaking a foreign language before I began school. I thought that learning a foreign language would be like learning a secret code. I would be able to understand talk that none of my friends or family could decipher. I could use a special language that no one else knew, or have secret conversations with someone who spoke the language. I persuaded two girls who lived next door to teach me French after they came home from school every afternoon. They enjoyed playing teacher and willingly cooperated. They would give me written notes with the numbers and days of the week written down. I was too young to read but that didn't matter—I asked my father to read what they had written. However, his pronunciation was nothing like what the girls had told me. I remember I kept telling him he was wrong and he kept telling me that he was reading what they had written.

When I was about six or seven years old, my father took a special training course related to his work. His method of consolidating what he had learnt was to come home and teach me his summary of the training program for that day after our evening meal. Although I was so young I still understood most of what he told me. (Or I thought I did.) One evening he came home and told me he had attended a special lecture on how to learn effectively. He explained that you have to link new information to information you already know. If the connection is strange, crazy or even a bit risqué, all the better. I never forgot this, and used this basic strategy all through school and college—especially for cramming before exams. I have applied it to study in general and also to learning a foreign language vocabulary. Using this method, my students have memorised more than a hundred words and their meanings inside an hour. I will introduce you to this approach in this book.

Incidentally, my father asked me where I got the idea for my study methods. I told him he had taught me when I was six years old. He said he remembered the course and teaching me at night, but he couldn't remember anything about the lecture on study methods (or even doing it) and said he had never used any of the methods himself.

I couldn't wait to start high school when I would begin to learn French in earnest. The idea of school had never been so exciting. It was a huge disappointment. No one in the school—even those who finished their final year with top marks in French—could actually hold a conversation in the language. We weren't taught to speak the language; we even had trouble reading it. Everyone complained about having to learn French. I was ashamed to admit I actually enjoyed it, though at the same time I was disappointed with the lack of progress.

It was hard to become enthusiastic about the French lessons. They began with grammar and conjugations of verbs—not much spoken language. The lessons seemed designed not only to result in failure, but also to engender dislike, if not hatred, for the subject. Still, French was my consistently best subject.

When I left school I bought some phonograph records that taught French and attended an evening class at my own expense. My progress was a hundred times faster than it had been in high school classes. We actually spoke the language; we studied the spoken language or dialogue rather than narrative. We used an Assimil course book as our textbook.

During this time I found an Assimil German language course in a second-hand record store. They were selling it cheaply because they didn't have the textbook for the course, just the audio material. I knew I could buy the book from my language school so I bought the records and then I bought the textbook from my school. I was speaking reasonable German inside two months. I had friends who spoke German so I tried my new skills out on them. They couldn't believe their Australian friend was speaking German.

In the meantime I had discovered a very cheap Russian course. I saw it in a shop window as I was walking past and couldn't resist it. At first I thought they must have made a mistake with the price — it was so cheap. I realised that the price was subsidised by the Russian government but that didn't matter; here was a genuine language course that I could use. I began to learn Russian. My progress was slower than with German, but I was speaking the language.

My wife and I booked a passage for Europe with Germany as our destination, so I was highly motivated to improve my German. I learnt German from my records (I had now recorded them on to cassette tapes) for six months and this was sufficient to get by quite well in Germany.

Two weeks before we left Australia I bought a course called *Italian for Travellers*. We were travelling on an Italian cruise liner to Europe so I thought Italian would help. The course was very cheap and contained cardboard recordings of the text. I copied them to cassette tape so they would last the distance and began learning. The program was called the Lewis Robins Reinforced Learning Method and I thought it was great. I practised what I learnt on my Italian friends and I was pleased that I had learnt so much so quickly and so easily. I was so pleased with the course that I bought the French, German and Russian versions as well. I think they cost $3.20 each at the time. They also had a *Spanish for Travellers* course but I wasn't interested in learning Spanish back then. I have regretted not buying it ever since. Each course began by teaching the words and phrases that would do the most good and give the learner the greatest flexibility in speaking the language. The sentences were spoken in context — they weren't just random phrases the authors thought would be useful. The importance of this approach is discussed in chapter 4. I have since incorporated the reinforced learning methods into my strategies for other areas of learning and teaching.

On the ship, our table waiter spoke little English and no one else spoke Italian, so I was nominated to be interpreter for the table. Our waiter took delight in helping me improve my Italian. He always brought me extra servings at meal times and looked after me, so my study of Italian paid off.

On arrival in Germany I visited the local library to read books on electronics in German to learn the vocabulary. I filled my notebook with the technical terms I thought I would need. I applied for a position with an international electronics firm and landed a job translating a technical English text into German. It was very hard work requiring long concentration, but I was able to do it and greatly improve my vocabulary. I translated the text (with the help of a technical dictionary) for a German engineer and he improved my translation into good German. This was the most intensive language course I have ever undertaken.

I worked for a company, designing and servicing language laboratories, and it was a dream job. The electronics was mainly logical thinking and problem solving, which I enjoyed immensely. I was paid to travel and I loved working with equipment to learn languages.

While we were in Europe I discovered I could learn Dutch, Swedish and Russian via short-wave radio, so I immediately wrote away to the stations for the free textbooks that went with the programs. I received a free phonograph record to go with the Dutch textbook and paid for a set of long-play records to go with the Swedish textbook. In my job, I was often away from home for several days at a time, visiting schools to work with their language laboratories, so evenings I would often ask if there were any foreign-language classes in the school that I could attend, and often sat in on Russian, French or Spanish classes of an evening.

Living in Europe gave me my first experience of conversing with someone in a language that neither of us spoke as our mother tongue. It was exciting for me, but for Europeans it is an everyday occurrence. We had very close friends in Poland, but we could only converse with them in German. I bought some excellent Polish courses in Poland, so that was the beginning of yet another language. One of my German friends criticised me for learning so many languages. 'You will never be completely fluent in any if you are going to learn so many. Wait until your German is perfect.' I thought about it, and I continued my studies.

I found in many countries that it was essential to speak the local language when travelling, because for many people, that is their only language. It should never be assumed that others will speak English.

I was driving on a freeway in Poland when a police officer flagged me down.

'You are fined 200 zloty,' he said.

'Why?' I asked.

'I can only tell you in Polish,' he said. 'Can you understand Polish?'

'No,' I said. 'Do you speak German?'

'No.'

'Do you speak Russian?'

'No, but I can tell you in French. Do you speak French?'

I said I did.

He told me, 'You were driving in the wrong lane. You were in the overtaking lane but you weren't overtaking anyone. That is a 200 zloty fine.'

I told him the slow lane was full of potholes and I was merely driving around them. It doesn't matter, he told me. The fine is 200 zloty. In western currency 200 zloty wasn't worth much, but he then fined an East German driver for the same offence and it took most of his holiday savings.

I worked for a year as an English teacher in a middle school and enjoyed the experience. I developed methods for teaching German children to pronounce English words without a German accent. I remember as a small child, sitting in my backyard near our side gate, experimenting with diphthongs. (A dipthong is a combination of vowel sounds pronounced as one syllable, as in 'boy', 'say' and 'loud'.) If I slowed down saying the diphthong I found the sound broke up into two vowel sounds. I would say the word 'day' very slowly. It would come out 'd-ah-ee'. The 'a' sound was like 'ah', which is the Australian pronunciation. All of this helped when I was teaching English. I used the method I discovered as a toddler of breaking diphthong sounds down to their components and taught them to the students as separate sounds rather than as a single sound as is the usual practice. I found this was highly successful. I told the German students the word 'day' is pronounced 'd-eh-i'. My own accent underwent change, as I had to teach Standard British English pronunciation. When I returned to Australia my brothers said I 'spoke like a foreigner'.

After we returned to Australia I enrolled as a student teacher. I thought it would be a good opportunity to put some of my methods of learning and teaching mathematics into practice. I have always felt I cheated my way through teachers' college because I based my assignments on the learning and teaching methods I had already developed. I felt I only put in half the effort of the other students in my class, but the effort had been made years before. The lecturers encouraged me to develop my methods further.

When I was given the opportunity to teach my learning and teaching strategies in other countries I was delighted. I spent some time in Canada and then I was invited to take part in a United States government program that was exploring ways of teaching to produce exceptional students. After my first mathematics book was published I was invited to teach my methods in Singapore. This aroused my interest in learning Chinese and Malay. When I was invited to conduct training programs in Kuala Lumpur, Malaysia, I jumped at the chance. I bought books and tapes to learn Malay. While I was in Malaysia teaching my mathematics methods I was learning Malay as fast as I could.

I have since downloaded a course in basic Malay from the internet and now use that as a basis, along with two cheap courses teaching Malay and newspapers and some children's magazines which I brought back with me from Singapore.

One of my earlier books, *Speed Mathematics*, has now been translated into Indonesian, so I will have to learn Indonesian as well to read it. I am keen to find out if the translation is better than the original. Indonesian is almost the same as Malay, so I get two languages for the effort of learning one.

My knowledge of Chinese is still hovering around nil but I am able to wish others a happy new year in Chinese. I learnt this from a *Dennis The Menace* comic. According to Dennis the Menace, the greeting is *gung hay fat choy*. People understood me when I first tried this out, but they told me I was saying it in Cantonese. I should speak in Mandarin, they said, so they taught me the Mandarin equivalent, *gong xi fa cai*, pronounced 'gong see fah chigh'. My knowledge of Mandarin is still very basic but I can observe the formalities.

I enjoy learning languages with strange alphabets. That is partly how I developed my strategies for teaching reading and literacy. When you learn a language like Russian, Greek, Hebrew or Arabic, you have to sound out every word. It can be discouraging at first but it isn't long before you develop a 'sight vocabulary'—a body of words you recognise immediately, without effort. All of my children are voracious readers. Now my grandchildren are avid readers, too, reading years ahead of their age level—they have all benefited from my methods.

I currently speak and understand about fifteen languages. This sounds rather a lot, but this figure is a little misleading: if you learn Malay, you can understand Indonesian; if you know Dutch you can understand Afrikaans, and so on. I understand some languages quite well and I would say I am fluent in them. With other languages I can get by and read articles in a newspaper or on the internet. I have done public speaking in German and French (and taught in a German school) and could probably speak in public from notes in several other languages. Using the methods described in this book, you will be able to master foreign languages, too.

Language learning should be an adventure and certainly should be fun. To quote Captain Jean-Luc Picard of the *Star Trek: The Next Generation* television series, 'We can make it so.'

Why learn a language?

one
ένα
un
eins
uno
одйн
satu
yksi

For me, learning a language is a way to really get to know a people. I enjoy sitting on a bus in a foreign country conversing with strangers in their own language. I am part of their environment, not just an observer. I remember sitting in a streetcar in Poland discussing politics with my fellow travellers and thinking, *I am getting first hand insight into the way Polish people think.* Sitting at the table with East Germans in their homes discussing religion and politics provided some of my great memories of the country. I think of the picnics I was invited to and the time I spent with families while we lived in Europe and I realise that this could never have happened if we hadn't spoken the language of our host country.

Learning someone's language is an act of friendship. It gives you insight into how they think. There is a thrill that comes with your first successful attempt to converse with someone in their own language; when you first discover you are thinking in their language.

It is different visiting a country when you understand the language. It is much more exciting to ask directions in the language, shop in the language, take a train or bus, book a hotel room, order a meal. And the knowledge of the language required for this is fairly basic.

One of the first sentences I learn in any language is, 'Excuse me. Do you speak . . .?' and then I learn the words for the languages I feel confident with. This helps when I get out of my depth: if an answer is complicated, or if someone replies by asking me something I don't understand.

In your own country, you will make friends among people who are flattered you are making the attempt to learn their language.

Reasons for learning a language

Most people who learn a language have compelling and urgent reasons for doing so. Usually it is for business reasons—we have to travel and we want to be able to communicate. It could be that you deal with people or companies who do business in a foreign tongue. It will help if you speak the language of your supplier or your head office. Maybe all the manuals are written in Swedish or Korean; it will help if you can read them.

Maybe you are travelling to a holiday destination where people speak a different language. You will gain far more from the experience if you can speak at least some of the language.

Or you may have romantic reasons for learning the language— a marriage or a relationship. Perhaps speaking Vietnamese or Italian will help you to understand your spouse and your spouse's family better. The language will introduce you to their culture.

Maybe you are studying or researching a topic on which most of the information is published in a foreign language. It will certainly help if you can go to the original sources. If you are studying overseas, you need a good knowledge of the language. (Although I do remember migrants to Australia arriving when I was a boy and they spoke no English—many of them were in my class at school and soon passed the rest of us in our studies. They learnt English remarkably quickly.)

It may be that you *have* to study a language, because you are studying a course that requires it. You have no say in the matter.

It could be for seemingly frivolous reasons: you like the sound of a language, you bought a cheap course in the language, you are interested in the origins of the language or your own language. You may just want to learn for the challenge or for the fun of it.

Learning a language will keep your brain young. It is a pleasant way to keep your mind in shape and get the brain working. Actually, Canadian psychologists released a report in 2004 which claimed that being bilingual or multilingual may help prevent some of the effects of ageing on brain function and delay the onset of Alzheimer's. (The report is available online at <www.apa.org/journals/releases/pag192290.pdf>.)

Learning more than one foreign language

If you have already studied a foreign language, either at school or because your family spoke it or you lived for a time in a place where another language was spoken, you will find it easier to learn your next language. You will get better with practice, because you learn how to go about it, as well as understanding how grammar works better and seeing similarities and recognising origins or derivations of words. For instance, if you have learnt French, you will find it easier to learn Spanish or Italian. If you have studied German, you will find it easier to learn Dutch or any of the Scandinavian languages. A knowledge of Russian will give you a head start with any of the Slavic languages.

Once, while visiting the Hanover library, I found a Yiddish course with a book and phonograph records so I checked it out. I took it with me to the electronics firm where I worked and said to my colleagues, 'Listen to this. Here is a Yiddish course I borrowed from the library.' We listened. Their immediate reaction was, 'Hey, we can understand Yiddish,' because Yiddish is like a dialect of German. The language actually derives from old German. There are German dialects that I have trouble understanding, and many Germans can't converse with their fellow countrymen because the dialects are unintelligible, but Yiddish seems to me to be easy to understand. (In the movie *The Frisco Kid*, the character played by Gene Wilder speaks in Yiddish to Amish people, but they can't understand him, and he can't understand them when they speak in German. I don't know why—I had no trouble following both sides of the conversation in the movie!)

Even if the new language you want to study doesn't belong to a language group you are familiar with, you will find you are still better prepared with each successive language that you study. Many people set out to learn one language and then find they are hooked. I look on each language as a new friend. It is fun getting to know your new friend better.

★ ★ ★

No matter what the reason, I assume you are motivated to learn a language (whether willingly or unwillingly). Whatever the reason, I will show you in the following chapters the easiest method to accomplish your goal.

Preparation

2

two
δύο
deux
zwei
dos
два
dua
kaksi

There is a proverb which I learnt as part of my German course, *alle Anfänge sind schwer*, or 'all beginnings are difficult'. The problem is, when we embark on a new project, we look at the whole task and it seems to overwhelm us. There is so much to learn. How will we ever do it?

This prevents many people from making the attempt. They never begin because the task looks impossible. This applies to language learning as it does to all areas of life. The best approach is to break up your study time into small periods and set yourself some goals.

Using your time well

Many books and websites tell you that you need to spend at least three hours a day working on your language or you are wasting your time. Not so. I spent no more than thirty minutes a day learning survival Italian and spoke the language reasonably well in two weeks. It was enough for the basics and it enabled my family and me to travel on an Italian ship and to survive in Italy.

I learnt German spending between twenty and thirty minutes a day for around six months. Each day's study was broken up into several chunks. I would spend five to ten minutes in the morning playing my lesson for the day on my cassette player and follow the text in my textbook. Then, at morning coffee, I would take out my textbook and read the lesson through. I would do this again in my lunch break and again at afternoon coffee break. I often commuted to work, so I would read the lesson through on the train morning and evening. Had I driven, I would have listened to the lesson in my car as well.

When I arrived home, I would play the tape again in the evening and read the lesson through one more time. Most of these sessions lasted five minutes and a maximum of ten to fifteen minutes. I was able to hold simple conversations with my German friends after around six weeks. After six month's study of around thirty to forty minutes a day, I was able to speak the language in Germany without difficulty.

By breaking my study time into small chunks of five to ten minutes I was easily able to reach my objective.

On weekends I would try to spend some extra time using my other tools. While I was walking by myself in the street I would talk to myself in German. I would talk to myself while I was driving. I would hold conversations with myself and try to construct the sentences by myself. I usually carried a small dictionary so I could look up any words I didn't know on the spot. This was the language I wanted to use and the language I needed—not the language that somebody else thought I should need or would be good for me to know.

So, I would ask for a daily commitment of half an hour broken up into small five-minute or ten-minute chunks spent on your 'target language' (the language you want to learn). This book will even give you a contingency plan for the days you just can't be motivated to spend even half an hour on your language studies. If you are highly motivated and want to spend more time—maybe you have a deadline—you can spend longer each day and learn the language even faster.

I will also show you how you can utilise 'lost' time—time you didn't know you had—to learn the language. The good news is that you don't have to take time from other activities to do most of your language learning.

You will be your own teacher

When you learn a language the fast, easy way, you must be your own teacher. This may seem like a strange concept. How can you teach yourself something you don't know? Shouldn't you find yourself a teacher who knows the language?

Here is what I mean by being your own teacher: *you will decide how you learn and what your learning materials will be.* You can take advice, but the decisions will be yours. You will not learn the language according to just one method—you will use several methods simultaneously. Instead of working your way through a single textbook or language course, you will use several textbooks and as many other language teaching aids as you can.

Instead of working at learning the language, you will enjoy yourself playing with the language. You can do this even if you are studying for a school or college examination. Instead of hard work, learning a language will be a pleasure.

Choosing a language

Have you chosen the language you want to learn? If you are going to work in Sweden, work with Swedish operating manuals, or you are going to marry a Swede, the choice is made for you.

If you are going to be working in Eastern Europe, you need to know which is the best choice of language for you. It could be German or Russian rather than the language of the country where your head office is situated. Ask other people which language will be most useful. Everyone's answer will be biased because his or her own language is always best. That is why your next question should be, 'If I learn a second foreign language as well, which would be most useful?'

If you are travelling through South America, should you learn Spanish or Portuguese? It depends where you will spend most of your time and which language will be most useful to you in the long run.

I have often studied languages just because I could. Tempt me with a good language program today and I will take it. Learning any foreign language will broaden your horizons.

So, choose your language and prepare for the adventure.

Setting goals

You should have clear goals when you make your decision to study a language. You should set yourself a long-term goal and also short-term goals as you go.

I am often invited to speak to professional groups. I give many after-dinner speeches and speak at sales breakfasts. I teach strategies for succeeding in life. The first rule of success in life is to set goals. First

I would like to give you my general advice on goal setting. There are three essential steps:

1. Determine what you want.

2. Make a plan to achieve it.

3. Put the plan into action.

It's as simple as that. This is the secret of success in a nutshell. Taking these three steps will put you ahead of most other people in any area of life.

When learning a language, step one is to choose the language. I will help you with the second step: together, we will work out a plan to learn the language. The third step is up to you. You will need to put the plan into action. I hope this book will motivate you to do that and also help you to stay motivated to keep learning the language—even when you don't feel like it.

Language goals

Your first goal is to choose the language. We have already discussed the issues involved in making this decision.

Next you must choose the level you want to reach. This is your long-term goal. The level you want to achieve will depend mainly on your reason for learning the language. If you are only making a flying business trip, you may not want to learn more than the basics. You will be surprised at what you can learn in a couple of weeks or a month. Your knowledge of the language can make a huge difference to what you personally get out of your visit.

If your aim is to be able to speak with clients who visit your business, you will want to learn more, but you won't necessarily want to be able to read the classics in the language. If you have to give a public presentation and speak to an audience in the language, you will need to learn it to a higher level than if you are just going to meet with local representatives of your company. If you are going to meet with technical people, you may decide you need to know the relevant technical terms.

If you are studying the language to pass an examination, your goals will be different. In fact, your college or exam will set your goals for you.

Most people choose to learn the language as well as they can, according to their circumstances. As circumstances change, we often have to change our goals. Many people decide that, after learning the basics, they want to learn the language better and continue their study long after they have achieved their original goal.

Time goals

It is always a good idea when setting goals to set yourself a deadline. For example, you might say to yourself, 'I want to be able to converse in basic Indonesian by the end of September,' or 'I want to be able to speak Swahili by the end of this year.' If your time limit is vague or open-ended, chances are you will never achieve your goal. If you use a language program, such as Assimil, your goals are already set out for you. Many courses break their material up into little chunks to be studied each day: you are able to determine beforehand exactly how long it will be before you finish.

Short-term goals

Next you need to set short-term goals. You might make it your goal to learn one lesson per day, or to spend forty minutes per day on your language study, split up into periods of five or ten minutes. You decide, but make sure your goals are realistic. There is no law that tells you that you can't change your commitment if you find you need more time or your circumstances change. It does help, though, to have some idea of what you can manage each day when you first make your commitment.

An early goal would be to master your survival language program. (We will talk about these programs in chapter 5.) You can set a goal for the date you want to achieve this. You will need to set further goals as you study the language. You might even make a commitment that the first thing you read each day will be in your target language. You can make the website of a newspaper in your target language your home page when you log on to the internet.

The advice in this book is understandably of a general nature. We are looking at learning any language, not one specific language. You might find you have to modify some of the suggestions in this book so they will work for you. Do so, by all means. It is the end result that is important. I have assumed in most cases that the language you are learning is a modern spoken language and not an ancient language, no longer in daily use, because we concentrate first on the spoken language. However, even if you are learning Ancient Greek, there are still many suggestions in the book you will find helpful.

Now, let's go to the next chapter and see what tools we will need for the job.

Choosing your tools

3

three
τρία
trois
drei
tres
три
tiga
kolme

Now that you have chosen your language, you will need some study aids. First, you are going to need a textbook. If you are studying a language at school you might have no choice in the matter—the textbook is chosen for you. We will do things differently; your set textbook is only one of your language tools.

Recorded language courses

There are language courses advertised that can cost anywhere between fifty dollars and several thousand dollars. The people who sell them tell you it is difficult to go out to a language class in the cold, wind, rain or snow. It is much easier, they say, to sit at home in your favourite chair, put on a CD or a tape, lean back with your eyes closed and learn with no effort … How is it, though, that so many of these courses are advertised for sale second-hand, hardly ever used? It is because it takes willpower to learn a language. There is effort involved. Be careful. Many people pay thousands of dollars to buy a language-learning program they think will do the job for them. An expensive program is no good if you don't use it. Also, the problem is that price is not always a reliable guide to the worth of a language program.

Would I recommend a complete language course? Yes, with a few reservations. There are some I would recommend, such as Assimil language courses. I would also recommend Transparent Language programs for your computer, but computer programs have a major disadvantage: you can only use them on your computer. You can't just take out your book or recording and learn wherever you are.

Try to buy a course, even if it is a cheap one, that is recorded entirely in the language you are learning. This will assist you to learn the correct pronunciation and 'music' of the language and also assist you to think in the language.

In any case, the course should not stand alone, but should be used in conjunction with other learning materials. I will say more on complete language courses in chapter 8.

Textbooks

First, you need a textbook. In fact, I recommend you purchase several. You should have at least two textbooks to begin; in fact, I would recommend having three. Then, if you come across other books that look helpful and interesting, buy them as well. This will give you a number of points of view of the language, and what you don't understand in one textbook might be quite clear in another. This is my advice for students studying any subject. We don't all learn the same way. A textbook explanation might make perfect sense to one person, while another learner might find it impossible to understand. This has nothing to do with intelligence, or even learning styles; the second person merely needs to have the material explained in a different way.

I would choose textbooks that teach spoken language as well as narrative. By spoken language, I mean dialogue. A story can be interesting to read, but it won't teach you the language you need to know to speak to someone, to ask directions or to buy a cup of coffee. Look for textbooks that include both narrative and dialogue.

The textbooks should explain first how the alphabet works. Although the language might be written in a familiar alphabet, each language has its rules of pronunciation. For instance, the *ch* sound in the English word 'chin' is written as *cz* in Polish, simply as *c* in Malay and Indonesian, and as *ce* or *ci* in Italian. Vowel sounds are usually different in different languages as well. You don't have to learn them all at once, but you should be able to read the rules and understand them from your textbook.

Learning the rules of grammar and pronunciation should help your understanding of your own language as well. Did you know there is a rule which determines when you pronounce *c* as a *k* or an *s* in English? The simple rule is, if *c* is followed by *i, e* or *y* it sounds like an *s*. Otherwise, it sounds like a *k*. Knowing the rules of pronunciation means you can read a word and say it. If you don't know the word, but you know how to pronounce it, you can at least ask, 'What does this word mean?'

The kinds of textbook to look for are those that have short chapters or lessons. They should have a short reading section to illustrate the grammar and vocabulary introduced in the lesson. There should be no more than three points of grammar covered in each lesson; otherwise you can become discouraged by the volume of information to learn.

The textbook should explain the grammar so that you can understand it. The best grammar explanations are those that occur throughout the text and explain it as you need it. It is good to have a grammar section at the end of the book. If not, buy a grammar book for the language you are learning—again, make sure you can easily understand it.

Your texts should have a maximum of around twenty or twenty-five new words per lesson. There should be a vocabulary on the page for all new words. Authors of many language textbooks seem to feel they are doing you a favour when they make it difficult to find the meaning of a word you don't know. They either put the vocabulary at the back or leave it out all together, expecting you to look the word up in a dictionary. Do they think that the more effort you make to find the meaning of a word, the more likely you are to remember it? A vocabulary at the back of the book is all right if it is there in addition to vocabulary on the page. If there is no vocabulary on the page, I would be inclined to reject the book and look for another. The time spent looking each word up is really time you are taking away from learning the language. Having the index in the back of the book, or not at all, means you waste time looking up words you don't know, which in turn means it takes longer to get less done. So, textbooks which explain new words as they are presented, on the same page, actually save you time—you learn the language faster and with less effort.

There are exceptions to this rule. I have an excellent Russian course which has a textbook for foreigners written in Russian, and a separate grammar and dictionary for speakers of various languages. The course was so good I decided to use it even though I had to use the separate English grammar book and dictionary, and I am glad I did. If you decide you like a textbook in spite of its shortcomings, buy it, but make sure you have other textbooks as well that will make your task easier.

Ideally, each textbook should give literal as well as colloquial translations. This gives you more words for your effort and lets you know how the language is put together. For instance, an Italian textbook might present an everyday phrase as follows:

Phrase:	*A che ora parte il treno per Firenze?*
Literal translation:	'At what hour leaves the train for Florence?'
Colloquial translation:	'When does the train leave for Florence?'

When the information is set out in this way, students not only learn the individual vocabulary words, but also learn about how sentences are put together in Italian.

There was a big move away from literal translations back in the sixties and seventies and I think it was a mistake. Even if it is just the odd note through the translation, it lets you know what the words mean and also makes you familiar with the language's word order.

Also, check that the lesson materials in the book will be interesting and useful to you. Some older textbooks were all narrative, and fairly useless narrative at that. Some of the newer school textbooks are superficial and are of little use for a business trip or for serious study of the language. However, if a book looks interesting, buy it along with other textbooks that will take you further with the language. If you have chosen a rather obscure language, you may not have much choice—you will have to make do with what you can get. A bad textbook is better than no textbook at all.

Dictionaries

You should buy two dictionaries: a small dictionary for travellers that will fit in your pocket and a good dictionary that will enable you to translate most texts and give grammatical information about each word. Make sure they are two-way dictionaries. If you are learning French, for example, then you will need a dictionary with both a French-English section and an English-French section to look up words either way. Check that this is what you are buying.

If you are learning a language which uses ideographs or symbols, like Chinese or Japanese, you may need to invest in several dictionaries. Students of Japanese, for example, may start out with a dictionary using familiar roman characters, but they will eventually need both a dictionary using the phonetic Japanese syllabaries and a 'character dictionary' which will allow them to look up unfamiliar characters whose sounds they do not know.

You can often find excellent dictionaries in second-hand stores or opportunity shops that have been discarded by students. Many second-hand bookshops and op-shops have sections in which they sell second-hand educational books. You can often buy an excellent dictionary or textbook for a fraction of the price you would pay for it new.

You might also need a technical dictionary if your work involves specialised language. If you are dealing with a specialist field, buy an appropriate dictionary. It can also be a good idea to buy a simple textbook on the subject or area you are working in, written in the language you are studying. That will give you much of the language you need to know. When I arrived in Germany, I needed to know words relating to science and electronics which weren't in most dictionaries. I read the technical books in the library and purchased a very simple textbook that dealt with my subject. I also bought an expensive technical dictionary and an inexpensive paperback technical dictionary that I could carry with me. That was more than enough for my purpose.

Phrasebooks

As well as your dictionary you need a phrasebook—maybe two. If you can buy a phrasebook that does the job and fits comfortably in your pocket, it may be sufficient. If it is bulky, buy yourself a small one as well.

The phrasebook should be relevant to what you need. Read the books in the bookstore before making your choice. Lonely Planet phrasebooks are excellent, giving both the phrases and advice on how to use them. They give useful information on the culture and help you avoid making embarrassing mistakes.

Once, when I was conducting a mathematics-training program in Kuala Lumpur, Malaysia, I was asked at the end of the program to give out diplomas to the graduating students. I had to shake the students' hands and give them their diplomas. Normally, in Australia, I would give the diploma with my left hand while I shook the right hand. Fortunately, I had read the Lonely Planet phrasebook I had just purchased, and I knew you never pass anything to anyone with your left hand in Malaysia. It is an insult. So, I handed a diploma to each student with both hands, and then I shook their right hand. That was the right way to do it. I asked my hosts what the reaction would have been if I had given the students their diplomas with my left hand. 'They would have just thought you were an ignorant foreigner,' was their reply. I was glad the phrasebook included not only phrases but also advice on how to use them.

A phrasebook with a recording of the phrases is a good choice. It not only teaches you what to say, but how to say it, too.

Also, look at the transliteration of the phrases—how the pronunciation is explained. Don't choose a book that uses international phonetics symbols unless you already read them fluently. Choose a book that explains how each word is pronounced simply and tells you which syllable has the stress (this is usually indicated in capitals or bold type). If a phrasebook has no pronunciation guide, or if it just refers you to the accompanying recordings, it is probably not a good choice.

Cassettes, CDs and MP3s

Audio recording technology is one of the great gifts to language learners and enthusiasts. In the past, language learners who couldn't find a native speaker to guide them had to rely on written descriptions of the correct pronunciation of words or phrases in their target language. Phonograph records changed that forever. Now you have the option of cassettes, CDs and, recently, digital audio files you can play on your computer, DVD player or a portable MP3 player.

If you have a cassette or CD that goes with your phrasebook, you don't really need any more recorded material, but the more recorded material you have, the easier it is to review what you have learnt and also to tune your ear to the language. You need to practise listening to the language as well as reading it. We will look at buying and choosing a complete recorded language course in chapter 8.

Children's recordings and stories are a good learning tool, especially if they have a written text to go with them. Any recorded text is good so long as it is clear and spoken with an authentic accent.

Also, seek out music recorded in the language you are studying. You can search for the lyrics on the internet. It is not difficult to find recordings of children's songs with a song book.

Portable cassette, CD or MP3 players

You can buy a cheap cassette player for less than $10 to listen to the language while you are walking or commuting. This will allow you to learn and review the language using time that would otherwise be lost. The same applies to portable CD players, which are inexpensive now and are useful for listening to audio CDs on the go.

If you have an MP3 player and you are able to convert recordings to the MP3 format on your computer, this is an excellent tool. You can fit hours of recorded material on your player and listen while you are walking, shopping or travelling.

Reading for pleasure

If you live in a large city, you can almost certainly buy newspapers and magazines in your target language. You will probably find a selection of foreign-language newspapers if you go to the larger distributors or newsagencies. Ask consuls or embassies if you can have some of their old, discarded newspapers and magazines if they don't mind. Usually they will be pleased to help. Otherwise, ask where you can buy them for yourself. You could ask your local newsagent to order them for you, or take out a subscription directly with the newspaper or magazine yourself.

You can always download articles from newspapers and magazines on the internet and print them for later study and translation practice. The articles and the advertisements will give you practice with the language you need to know.

Foreign-language bookshops can usually assist you with fun reading materials. Many carry comic books and magazines in a variety of languages. You can buy Tintin comics in almost any language. Look for joke books. A good choice is a book of cartoons with one short punchline— you won't get discouraged looking up the words in a dictionary.

If you are religiously inclined you can study your religious texts in your target language. You can often get these for free; otherwise the cost is usually small. You can download Bible texts in many languages for free from the internet. You can also download the Bible on audio files in many languages so you can follow the spoken word with the text.

When I was staying in Singapore, I found a Buddhist 'Gideon Bible' in the bedside drawer of my hotel room. It advertised that you could receive a free copy of the book in a number of languages from an address nearby. I got my free English copy and was charged a small fee for a copy of the teachings of Buddha in Russian.

Internet

The internet offers a wealth of material in just about any language. You can visit webpages in your target language and download articles to read and audio files to listen to. Newspaper sites are especially useful—you can print the news headlines for the day in the language you are learning. Each headline will be short and relevant to daily life. You can also find sites designed to help language learners. It is not difficult to find sites that give an introduction to the language. I found a complete course in the Malay language that I downloaded and now use. I will cover using the internet as a learning tool in chapter 18.

Radio and television

In Australia we have a huge choice of languages we can hear on the radio and watch on television. Films on SBS have subtitles at the bottom of the screen—you can check your understanding as you go. If you have an opportunity to see a movie a second time, watch it with the subtitles covered. With cable and satellite television you can receive programs from all parts of the world. Otherwise, buy videos you can watch on your video player—just make sure the videos you purchase are compatible with your country's television and video system. (In Australia, PAL is the most common system; to watch videos made in some other countries you may need a special video player.) DVDs are another good option. You can choose to watch movies in your target language with or without subtitles, or even English-language movies dubbed into other languages. Again, you must check that a DVD is appropriate to your region.

The internet has made foreign-language broadcasts available to anyone. You can search for a radio station which broadcasts on the web in the language you are learning and hear a good quality reception.

Flashcards

You can make your own flashcards to review words you are currently learning or words that give you difficulty. You can make your own plastic holder if you can't find one in a stationery store. I use an old diary cover to hold my cards. Flashcards are suitable for learning the days of the week, numbers (from one to ten at first and then to one hundred), colours and so on. I find flashcards most useful for these kinds of lists and for specialised words such as the names of chess pieces, medical or technical terms and the like. They can also be very useful in learning languages such as Chinese or Japanese, which use large numbers of characters that must be memorised. I have seen differing opinions about flashcards—some language enthusiasts oppose them completely. I say, try them and see how they work for you. We don't all think the same way and, if they work for you, by all means use them.

Notebooks

Buy yourself three or four notebooks you can devote just to your language study. You will make your own notes from your textbooks and write your exercises in the first notebook. The second notebook will be for general vocabulary. A third notebook can be used for sentences, phrases and vocabulary that are important to you. The fourth notebook will be used as your survival language textbook.

Studying at school or for an examination

If you are studying a language for an examination or for school, use the methods described above as far as possible. Your school or course textbook will be your main text, but it will not be your only learning tool. A big difference between you and the other students in your class is that you will take control of how you learn the language. You are working to your own agenda.

Make language learning fun. This takes the stress out of learning for an examination. Play with the language. Read your joke books and comics. Listen to music. Visit places where the language is spoken. Other students are working at the language; you are playing at it. Enjoy it.

Tools: a summary

Here is a list of basic tools you will need to study your language:

- language textbooks—general

- dictionary

- phrasebook

- cassettes or CDs

- school readers or children's books

- newspapers and magazines

- joke books and comics

- portable cassette, CD or MP3 player

- internet access

- flashcards

- children's story cassettes or CDs, especially those accompanied by a text

- cassettes or CDs of children's songs

- notebooks

Now you are ready to begin your adventure.

Getting started

four
τέσσερα
quatre
vier
cuatro
четыре
empat
neljä

Learn how to read the language

The first step in learning your target language is to learn how to read it. You need to know what sound the letters or letter combinations make. The letters may look familiar but may have quite a different sound in the language you are studying.

In Malay and Indonesian, *c* is pronounced like the English sound 'ch'. It is pronounced as *k* in Spanish, or like the English sound 'th' if it is followed by *i* or *e*. *Cz* is pronounced as 'ch' in Polish, and *sz* is pronounced as 'sh'. *W* is pronounced like the English letter *v* in many European languages. In German, *eu* is pronounced like 'oy'. This means that the word *Europa* (Europe) is pronounced 'Oy ROPE ah'. You need to learn the consonant and vowel sounds. Then, when you read an unfamiliar word, you can at least ask somebody, 'What does … mean?'

When I was learning German I was able to read aloud from written texts, much to the amazement of my German friends. It sounded like I had a knowledge of their language way beyond my ability. I was able to read texts in Polish to my friends in Poland, even though they knew my knowledge of their language was minimal at the time.

Most basic textbooks will give this information either in the introduction, or the first chapter of the book. I would read the explanation in at least two textbooks. You don't have to memorise all of the information; the knowledge will come quickly as you learn the language.

It is essential to follow the recorded text from your cassettes or CDs to learn the authentic pronunciation. You are not concerned with understanding at this stage, just learning the sounds of the language and how the written language corresponds with the spoken language. One advantage of learning most languages other than English is that they are pronounced pretty much as they are written. I have heard Germans complain about German spelling, and Russian has its quirks, but generally, spoken languages follow the written. In any case, even with English, you need to know the rules of spelling and pronunciation.

Try reading texts out loud, just for practice. You don't need to understand a word you are saying.

Learning from your textbooks

Once you feel comfortable with the spelling and pronunciation, it is time to start the language. Read the first two or three chapters in several textbooks. Read the foreign text aloud. The content will probably be fairly similar. This is good. Firstly, the repetition helps, and the differences in the explanations may also help you to understand better.

At this stage, I would only do a couple of examples from the written exercises in the books, or I might just do a couple of examples mentally or speak them aloud. Serious work with the exercises will come later.

The first lessons will explain some of the basics of the language. In some languages there are no 'articles'; that is, no word for 'a' or 'the'. 'A book' or 'the book' is just 'book'. Context tells you which it is. Many languages have 'gender' for all nouns. 'Table', for example, may be masculine or feminine or neuter. Don't look on these differences as problems but as an adventure.

I note anything I don't understand in my textbook with a pencil line down the side of the text and draw a star or asterisk alongside. Then I flip forward a few pages and note the page number with the difficulty in pencil down the side of the page. Then, when I have read a few more lessons I am reminded to turn back to my difficulty to see if it has been resolved. If it hasn't, I can make another attempt.

The fact that I am working with several textbooks means when I find a difficulty in one textbook, I am likely to read a different explanation in the others, which might make more sense and resolve the problem. If it still isn't resolved, I mark it even further ahead in my textbook and also make a note in my notebook so I can ask somebody who knows the language.

If your textbooks start explaining conjugations (the different forms verbs take) at this stage, read the explanations, but don't try to learn the different forms off by heart. You only need to recognise them at this stage.

Two waves

The approach I have just described briefly above is one I learnt from my Assimil language courses. Study your textbooks in two 'waves'. The first wave consists of reading through the chapters at a fast pace and reading the set exercises, but not necessarily doing them. You can try a couple of examples, either in your head or out loud, to see that you understand the idea, but that is all. You read the grammar explanations and the rules for conjugations of verbs but you don't worry about memorising them. You are only concerned about recognising the rules at this stage.

During the first wave you push the pace as fast as you can. You are only concerned about recognising and understanding at this stage. You should concentrate on understanding the written text and also understanding the spoken language on your recordings. You don't worry if you remember the vocabulary or if you keep forgetting the meaning of words. You simply push ahead and the meaning of words will come to you with repetition.

You begin the second wave after around six to eight weeks of study. While you are pushing ahead with chapter ten or twenty in the first wave, you go back to chapter one for your second wave study. This time you do the exercises, both written and oral, and try to translate from English to the foreign language. You read the grammar explanations again; this time they should not only make better sense than before, you should find them easy because you have been applying them for the last two months. The first wave is passive learning and the second wave is active.

Using the phrasebook

Now take out your phrasebook for travellers. Read the basic expressions and say them aloud. The book probably begins with greetings and polite expressions like, 'Hello', 'Goodbye', 'Please', 'Thank you', 'I am sorry', 'Excuse me' and 'Where is the toilet?' Say them aloud several times a day and they will soon become part of your knowledge of the language.

Write the important phrases and any phrase that might be particularly important to you in your notebook. I would add 'question' words like 'where', 'when', 'how', 'why' and 'what'. Prepositions are also important. They are words like 'in', 'out', 'inside', 'outside', 'near', 'over', 'under', 'above', 'below', 'to' and 'from'. You can draw a diagram to illustrate the meaning of these prepositions. An example is given in figure 4.1.

Figure 4.1: example of a diagram illustrating prepositions

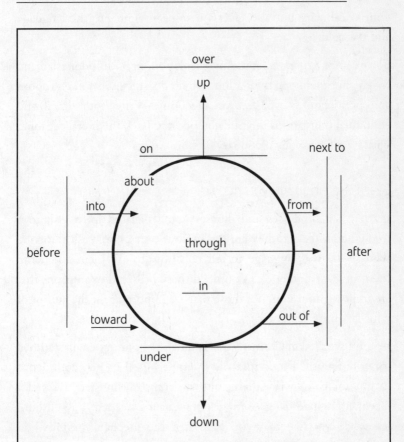

Also add phrases like, 'What is that?', 'What is this?', 'This is a …', 'How much?', 'How many?', 'Do you have?', 'How much does it cost?', 'Please pass the…' and 'Please write that down'.

You don't have to memorise them all at once. Reading them aloud at least once a day will soon put them in your permanent memory. I would try to do this early in the morning and last thing at night. Make some kind of a schedule.

As you write and learn the phrases, check the literal meaning of each phrase as well as the colloquial meaning. This will not only build your vocabulary but also give you some insight into the language and the culture.

For instance *terimah kasih* means 'thank you' in both Indonesian and Malay, but the literal translation (which doesn't appear in textbooks and phrasebooks) is 'Receive affection'. Write both literal and colloquial translations in your notebook. Check the literal meaning with help from your dictionary.

Learn the language you need

If there are sentences and phrases you will need for a visit to a foreign country and they are not in your phrasebook, ask someone who speaks the language to tell you how to say them and write them in your notebook. You need the words and expressions that are important for you, not those that are important for the author of your language textbook.

When I worked in Germany as a language laboratory engineer I had to write reports. I tried to avoid them because I had no confidence in my ability to write them, but the company insisted. I asked a German engineer to give me the sentences I needed. I asked him, 'How do you say that you calibrated the mechanism? How do you say you checked all units?' I knew how I would *say* all of this talking to someone face to face, but I wanted to make sure I was writing it in correct German. I wrote a page of these sentences and I also copied the report he had just written on the work we had just done. Using my notes as a guide, I found I was able to write excellent reports on my work; in fact, my written reports were probably in better German than my oral reports. There are only a limited number of things to write in this kind of report, whether it be technical, medical or sporting. I could take the basic sentence, 'Replaced damaged diode', and make it, 'Replaced damaged capacitor', 'Replaced damaged transistor', 'Replaced damaged IC', or 'Replaced damaged resistor'. A dozen or so basic sentences were enough for me to describe almost anything that I had to do to repair a language laboratory system. After my first two or three reports, I never had to refer to my notes again. I just needed to be pushed into writing reports. I was glad of it later—it wasn't as bad as I had feared.

Using your notebooks

As I said earlier, I would keep three notebooks, or more if you wish. I have one for working with my textbooks and any written exercises; I write my vocabulary words in the back, noting where the word first appears in the textbook. I list a word as 'A3' or 'B5', meaning textbook A, lesson 3 or textbook B, lesson 5. Once you have started doing this, you should revise your lists. Read them through on a regular basis. You may like to keep your vocabulary in a separate notebook.

In another notebook I write my own notes and phrases that I want to learn. This is *my* language book. I write the days of the week in this book. I also write numbers, colours and how to tell the time. There are some things you need to know to survive. Write them all in your notebook. 'Please call a doctor or an ambulance' could save your life.

I remember standing at a bus stop shortly after I arrived in Germany. A man was standing on the road at the other end of the stop with his back to the traffic. I saw the bus coming and thought the man's position was possibly dangerous, so I went to call out a warning to him. I couldn't think of the German for 'Look out' or any other appropriate warning. While I was still trying to formulate something to call out in German the bus hit the man on the shoulder and he fell to the ground, injured. Because of this, I would add the warning 'look out!' to my vocabulary list, and also the word for 'help'.

Two interpreters were standing at the railing of a ship. 'Can you swim?' asked one.

'No, but I can call for help in nine different languages,' replied the other.

Write your special vocabulary in this notebook as well. Those are the words and phrases you will need for your own purposes. If you are a footballer you will need football vocabulary; if you are going to play chess, you must learn chess terms; and if you are learning a language for business reasons you will need to know special vocabulary connected with your business. It all goes in your notebook.

The 80/20 rule

In 1906, Italian economist Vilfredo Pareto created a mathematical formula to describe the unequal distribution of wealth in his country, observing that twenty per cent of the people owned eighty per cent of the wealth.

After Pareto made his observation and created his formula, many others observed similar phenomena in their own areas of expertise. The 80/20 rule is usually applied to time management, to sales and other areas of business. The idea is that 80 per cent of sales are made by 20 per cent of a business's salespeople. Twenty per cent of our time produces 80 per cent of our results—the other 80 per cent of our time is virtually nonproductive. Twenty per cent of your items on sale account for 80 per cent of your sales.

This principle can be applied to learning a language: twenty per cent of words in a language make up 80 per cent of conversations and writing. Actually, the ratio is even greater. Learn just one thousand major words in a language and you can converse on most topics and make your meaning known. Young toddlers get across a lot of meaning with very few words.

You don't want to speak like a toddler, but you can be remarkably fluent in a language by learning the right words and phrases. If you choose even one hundred strategic words you can say a lot. I have read that the 100 most common words in a language make up fifty per cent of any conversation. These are the words you want to learn first, and then build on this foundation.

Choose your vocabulary

When you learn 'survival' language, you should learn the useful, high-frequency words first. After you learn basic greetings and polite expressions you should learn the words and phrases that will do you the most good. That is how I learnt to speak useful Italian in just two weeks.

I would suggest starting with basic words and the phrase 'I would like...' This is a handy phrase to learn in any language. You can use it to say, 'I would like a room', 'I would like a cup of coffee', 'I would like to see Mr Smith', 'I would like to go to Paris', 'I would like to eat in a French restaurant' and so on. Incredibly, I was never taught this important phrase in the first three or four years of French at high school because it involved the conditional form of the verb, yet it is very simple: *je voudrais*. There is no need to understand how the conditional is formed to use this phrase and be understood. This should be one of the first phrases you learn in your target language:

- In German it is *ich möchte*.

- In Italian it is *vorrei*.

- In Russian it is *ya bi khotel*.

- In Spanish it is *me gustería*.

Find out how you say it in the language that you are learning—it may be very simple.

In the same category I would list 'I need ...', 'I like ...' and 'I want ...' These are useful phrases to learn, because, in many languages, you don't have to know all of the forms of the verbs that follow, only the infinitive. This gives you a lot of scope.

Add to this list the verbs:

to have	....
to go	....
to go to	....
to speak	....
to speak with	....
to understand	....
to see	....
to eat	....
to drink	....
to open	....
to close	....

Then add the nouns:

a room (with a bath/shower) ....

a table (for one/two) ....

a taxi ....

a car ....

a doctor ....

You can now say: 'I would like a room', 'I need a doctor' or 'I would like a room with a bath'. You can also say 'I would like to speak with Mr Smith', 'I would like to go to Milan', 'I would like to see the manager' and 'I would like to eat in my room'. Note that in many languages, when 'I would like' is followed by a verb, it is always the infinitive—you don't have to know all of the forms of the verb to say what you want.

Some more useful, high-frequency words to learn are listed over the next few pages:

I ....

you (singular) ....

he ....

she ....

it ....

we ....

you (plural) ....

they ....

with me ....

with you ....

now ....

soon ....

later ....

immediately ....

today ....

tomorrow ....

yesterday ....

if ....

when ....

good ....

bad ....

easy ....

difficult ....

very ....

more ....

less ....

left ....

right ....

High-frequency phrases are also useful:

Do you have ...? ....

Where is ...? ....

Can I? ....

Is it possible? ....

May I? ....

Is it allowed?	....
Please write it down for me.	....
Please pass the butter/salt/etc.	....
Please speak more slowly.	....
My name is ...	....
What is your name?	....
Please write that down.	....
Why?	....
Because...	....

Write them all in your notebook. This is much more useful than the approach of most language textbooks.

In Latin-derived languages, such as French, Spanish and Italian, there is a shortcut for learning the future tense. You don't have to know the future tense of each verb. Instead, you can preface your sentence by saying, 'I am going to ...' to announce your future intention:

- I am going to play.

- I am going to see Mr Smith tomorrow.

- I am going to eat in the hotel.

- I am going to buy a ticket.

Again, you are using the infinitive form of the verb. This doesn't work with all languages—find out whether there is an equivalent strategy you can use in your target language.

Learning the above words and phrases will have you speaking intelligible, practical sentences in less than a week. This is much better than learning nonsense phrases such as 'The pen of my aunt is on the bureau of my uncle.'

You may not understand everything that is said to you, but you can say what you want to get your point across. You cannot control other people's vocabulary when they speak to you but you can certainly control your own. When I am in the learning stage of a language I can usually get my meaning across; if not directly, at least I can do it indirectly. I may have to talk 'around' something because I don't know the correct words to use, but I can usually find some way to say what I want. Treat such situations as an adventure. Then, when the person you are speaking to has understood what you are trying to say, ask how you should have said it.

I try to anticipate the difficulties and deal with them in advance by holding pretend conversations with myself in the language. When I find there is a word or phrase I don't know, I can look it up or ask somebody who speaks the language, *before* I need it. Then I write it in my notebook.

You will also want to learn the numbers, colours and days of the week. You need to be able to understand and to say the time; you need to understand numbers to know how much you need to pay. Put it all in your own language notebook and revise what you have written every time you get the chance.

Formal or informal

Most languages have a formal and an informal mode of address. There is an informal way to address people you know quite well, members of your family and young children. There is another formal mode of address used to speak with people you don't know so well.

In French the informal and the formal words for 'you' are different: the informal word is *tu* and the formal word is *vous*. In German, they are *du* and *Sie*. In both of these languages, the choice of pronoun — formal or informal — will affect the form of the verb you must use. You should definitely learn to use formal language first, but you should recognise the informal. Make sure you understand the difference, and that you know what you are saying. Using the wrong form can cause great offence. Many languages have several different levels of formality. Malay, for example, has various forms of address, and both Chinese and Japanese use a complex honorific system to pay respect to people spoken to or spoken about. Find out what is appropriate in your target language by consulting native speakers.

Alphabet

You need to learn the names of the letters of the alphabet in your target language, because you will often be asked, 'How do you spell that?' The language you are studying might use the same alphabet you know, but I can guarantee that the names of the letters will be pronounced differently.

People will ask you to spell your name. You should be able to spell your name without hesitation, so practise until you have memorised it. You will also have to ask people how to spell their name. People will often spell words out for you. You can always ask them to write unfamiliar words down, but you will still need to know how the names of the letters are pronounced. Once, when we lived in Germany, I had to telephone for an ambulance. We lived in Selma Street (*Selmastrasse*) and I had difficulty pronouncing the German *l*. I had to spell out the name of the street on the phone to be understood. It is a very important skill to have.

Bribe yourself

To keep on track, set targets for each day. For example, you might tell yourself, *today I will complete lesson 14 in my textbook and translate three jokes*. Promise yourself a treat on completing your task—bribe yourself to achieve: *when I finish the first twenty lessons I will treat myself to …* Your treat could be anything from a meal at a restaurant serving food from your target language culture to a new CD in the language, or just a day off to enjoy yourself. Bribery is one way to motivate yourself to achieve more.

Have a contingency plan for the days you feel totally unmotivated, perhaps something like: *If I just can't work up the energy to look at my textbook, I will listen to a language tape while I am doing my chores or driving my car.* Listening to your tape may do the trick of motivating you anyway. Have something definite planned that you think will work for you.

★ ★ ★

You are now well on your way towards achieving your goal. In the next chapter, I am going to show you how you can make your own survival language course. This will be a central part of your study of the language and will enable you to reach your goal of speaking and understanding the language faster than most courses or textbooks would, and you will have put together the survival course yourself—it will be *your* course, dealing with the language that *you* think is important.

Make your own survival course

5

five
πέντε
. cinq
fünf
cinco
пять
lima
viisi

I have already mentioned the survival Italian course I completed in two weeks before my family and I travelled to Europe. It worked because it was written in dialogue form. Materials were presented almost as several short stories or situations, easy to identify with. It also worked because the words chosen were those that joined the language together—basic words like 'I', 'you', 'we', 'and', 'the', 'on' and 'with'. It also taught the useful phrase, 'I would like ...'

You can make a shortened version of the program for yourself. If you have not yet bought yourself a notebook for this purpose, do so now. Firstly, write down imaginary conversations in English that you might encounter on your visit to the country. Begin with the border crossing and customs. Leave plenty of room for further notes. It should look something like this:

English	German
Where can I find a bank?	Wo kann ich eine Bank finden?
	Where can I a bank find?

As you can see, I have suggested that you write the English sentences down the left-hand side of the page. You should make sure there is enough space for the foreign translation on the right. Below each English sentence, leave enough room for a literal translation of the foreign sentences on the right. Writing the literal translation of the foreign sentence gives you an expanded vocabulary as well as showing you how sentences are constructed in your target language.

If you were in a shopping centre and asked somebody, 'Where bank?' I am sure you would be understood, even if you couldn't remember the full sentence. Learning your survival language will take you a long way.

To get started, imagine yourself arriving in the country, and mentally run through the conversations you will need to survive. First, write in the English.

Next, write the translation of each sentence in your target language, and then write the literal English translation of what you have written. You will probably need a native speaker of the language to help you with this. Use your phrasebook to find as many of the phrases and sentences as possible. I used the 101 Languages of the World computer program by the Transparent Language Company to write and translate my own booklet of survival Malay. The entries in your booklet might look something like the example given opposite in figure 5.1.

In appendix A, you will find several pages of model phrases, sentences and conversations. You can photocopy it for your own use as a survival course book, if it meets your needs, or alternatively, use it as a basis for the development of your own booklet, adapting the material to suit your own purposes. It might be a good idea to break the sections of your survival language book into sections of around ten to twenty sentences for easy revision. Try to make natural breaks so each section contains one or two conversations.

Figure 5.1: example of a model survival course conversation

English	Target language
Good day. Can I help you?	....
	....
I would like to see Mr Smith.	....
	....
I have an appointment with Mr Smith.	....
	....
Is Mr Smith here?	....
	....
I will see if he is free.	....
	....
He is here.	....
	....
He will be with you shortly.	....
	....

Read your language guide through on a daily basis, speak it aloud and change the sentences—practise substituting words according to your own imaginary situations, and you will survive quite well.

The next step is to make a recording of the text of your book. If you have a friend who is a native speaker of the language, ask him or her to read the text aloud into a tape recorder. You may be able to persuade a native speaker to record it for a small fee. Just ask them to read the foreign text—don't put the English translation on the tape. Failing that, you can always record yourself reading the text. Then you can play the tape on a daily basis and easily make the phrases part of your working knowledge of the language. This is a great start to learning the language. You have learnt phrases and a vocabulary that is both important and useful for further language study. It gives you something to build on.

If you have broken your survival guide up into sections, make each section a task for one day's revision. Then, when you have completed learning all of the sections, you can maybe break the book up into two halves and revise a whole half each day for a week or so, then every few days. I have found this method very effective.

Even if you are only making a short visit for a holiday, mastering the survival language will add a lot to your enjoyment of your visit and allow you to do much more than you would on a guided tour.

Learning a different alphabet or writing system

6

six
έξι
six
sechs
seis
шесть
enam
kuusi

When you learn a language like Russian, Greek, Arabic or Hebrew, you are not only faced with the task of learning the language, you have to learn a whole new alphabet as well. It discourages many people from even making a beginning. I have had this experience several times. The problem is not as bad as it seems. It won't be long before you are fluently reading the language.

Here is how I suggest you go about it. Firstly, your textbook should only introduce a few letters at a time. My first Russian textbook was called *My First Russian Book*. It introduced a couple of letters that were the same in English and Russian and a couple of new letters in the first lesson. The sentences were so easy it seemed that learning Russian would be a breeze. It began in Russian, 'This is Tom', 'This is Nina', 'This is Mama', 'This is Papa', 'This is a house'. It was easy. Then it asked, 'Is this Tom?' 'Is this Nina?'

It was all easy stuff, and the alphabet was a minor item because most of the letters were familiar.

The next lesson introduced some more letters, and so on, until I learnt all of the letters in the Russian alphabet and hardly noticed it. Who says you have to learn them all at once?

When the alphabet or writing system is entirely different

If you are learning Greek or Russian, most of the letters will be fairly familiar. Some letters look the same but have different values or pronunciation to the English letter. For example, the symbol *H* represents an *n* sound in the Russian and Greek alphabets. The name 'Anna' would be written in Russian 'AHHA'. The Russian letter *Y* sounds like the English letter *u,* so the word *TYT* (meaning 'here') is pronounced 'toot'. The Russian letter *B* sounds like the English letter *v,* so *BOT* sounds like 'vawt' (meaning 'here is'). It doesn't take long to learn and you will soon get used to it.

If you are learning Sanskrit, Arabic or Hebrew, or any other language in which there is no similarity between the appearance of the letters you have to learn and your own alphabet, you should restrict yourself to just learning a few letters at a time. A good textbook will take this approach. They often write names and international words that you recognise in the foreign alphabet you are learning to give you practice sounding out the letters and words.

You can find foreign-language alphabet lessons and charts on the internet. For the Sanskrit, Arabic, Russian, Greek, Tamil and Hebrew alphabets, I recommend a visit to <www.ukindia.com>. This site has files 'zipped' for easy downloading, so you can view them on your computer. They give examples of familiar words spelt with the new alphabet to give you practice learning the alphabet symbols. Many sites have easy helps to enable you to learn the sounds of the alphabet.

You can also pick up alphabet books for children in religious shops that sell Hebrew, Arabic or Sanskrit books. It doesn't matter if the explanations are juvenile if they do the job.

When I am learning an unfamiliar script, I usually look for objects that the letters resemble that might remind me of the sound they make, or how they are pronounced. I try to make pictures of the letters or make the letter look like something familiar that begins with the appropriate English letter.

To give an example, I have seen an explanation for children on how to remember the two vowel sounds of the Hebrew letter *vav*. *Vav* looks like a vertical line. It is a consonant that sounds like an English *v*, but it can also serve as a vowel. This transformation is accomplished by adding a dot to the letter. If the dot is on the top, it is pronounced 'oh'; if it is halfway up the left side it is pronounced 'oo'. How do you remember it? Picture the dot as a ball. If it hits you on the head, you say, 'Oh', but if it hits you in the stomach you say, 'Ooh'. This is illustrated in figure 6.1.

Figure 6.1: the Hebrew consonant *vav* transformed into a vowel

sounds like 'v'   sounds like 'oh'   sounds like 'ooh'

This is how children are taught to remember and is the kind of strategy that you can use to make the learning of a different alphabet easier. Use your imagination to come up with your own ideas to remember the alphabet—especially the letters that keep giving you trouble. Experiment. Make your own connections with the letters and the sounds they make.

Chinese characters

If you are studying either Chinese or Japanese, you have the huge task of learning Chinese characters. (The Japanese 'borrowed' the Chinese writing system and adapted it to their own language.) What is the easiest way to do it? Here are my suggestions:

First, learn the logic of the symbols. They are not randomly designed. The symbols have meaning in the way they are constructed.

Once, when I was at a New Year's celebration, a Chinese woman sitting next to me decided to explain the Chinese characters. She showed me the symbol for 'person': 人. Then she drew a horizontal line through the symbol so it looked like this: 大. It looked like a man with his arms spread wide. 'It means "big"' I said, and I was right. It made sense. If you can learn the meaning of the symbols and follow the reasoning behind them they are much easier to learn.

If you can't understand or find any logic behind the symbols, make your own logic. Make up any meaning that will make sense to you. Say to yourself: 'This character looks like someone with a strange hat swinging a golf club.' Then create a crazy connection to help you remember its meaning and you will have it. (I explain this method of learning vocabulary in chapter 9.) Sure, it takes time and effort to do, but it is still easier than trying to memorise the symbols by rote.

There are excellent books available that teach the characters using the above methods. Search the internet as well. There are a number of sites with animated instructions on how to draw the Chinese characters. One I would recommend checking out is On-line Chinese Tools, at <www.mandarintools.com>.

Transliteration

If a textbook you are considering using expects you to learn the whole alphabet before you begin with the language, at least make sure it has a good transliteration with the text—an easy to understand pronunciation guide alongside the foreign script text—so that you can read without checking the alphabet page for every word. If the textbook doesn't have this, dump it, at least until you have progressed far enough that you don't need help with pronunciation.

The good news is that when you have progressed with the language you will no longer have to sound out every word—the words will be in your 'sight vocabulary'. This is how we should learn to read English. We should sound out the words we don't know until they enter our sight vocabulary. Until we do recognise the words at a glance, we have a strategy to read them anyway.

While you are still at the sounding out stage with the alphabet, don't be discouraged. You will progress to recognising the words at a glance and it will be sooner rather than later.

Reading texts and listening to texts while you follow the printed text will enable you to get used to the alphabet quickly. Remember, repetition is the key to fast learning of this kind.

I would look for a textbook or a page on the internet that teaches the alphabet to speakers of English. Often they will have memory pegs to help you learn the sounds of the alphabet that won't be in your regular textbooks. Use anything that you can.

Learn to recite the alphabet

When I learnt Russian I learnt the letters of the alphabet a few at a time. That made it easy for me to master the sounds of the letters and enabled me to learn the strange alphabet easily and without pain or effort. Unfortunately, though, it didn't teach me the order of the letters in the alphabet, so I had trouble looking up words in a dictionary. This is why you need to be able to recite the alphabet. You don't have to learn it immediately—you will have enough trouble in the first place just deciphering the strange letters and reading the words they form—but learning to recite the alphabet should be your next step.

You don't need to hurry this process. Begin with the first four or five letters of the alphabet, then the final letters and some of the middle letters. That will be enough at least to tell you to begin looking at the beginning or end of your dictionary for a word you don't know. Another idea is to mark the letters of the alphabet on the edge of the tightly closed pages of your dictionary. That will enable you to find words quickly.

The same principle applies to languages such as Korean which use a phonetic syllabary rather than an alphabet . Once you have learnt the order in which the at-first unfamiliar symbols are ordered, it will be much easier to use your dictionary.

Soon, you will be reading pages in the foreign text as easily as you do in your own language. You will wonder that you were ever troubled by the strange text.

Using a dictionary

7

seven
επτά
sept
sieben
siete
семь
tujuh
seitsemän

When my book, *Speed Mathematics*, was translated into Indonesian, I tried to translate the webpages that advertised it into English with the help of a dictionary. I was disappointed with the results. Most of the words just weren't there to be found.

When you use a dictionary to look up the meaning of a word you don't recognise, you will find that many words are not listed. That is because dictionaries give the basic or root form of a word and then list variations under this root word. Verbs, for example, are generally given in their infinitive form. If you look up the word 'seen' in an English dictionary, you will find it under the entry for the root verb, 'see'. The words 'is' and 'was' are found under the entry 'be'.

It is often difficult to find the word you want if you don't know the root word it is listed under. One way around this is to buy a large dictionary that lists words in their many forms and directs you to the appropriate root word to find the meaning of the word you want.

If you have just started learning French, how are you to know that *vais* and *va* are to be found under *aller*? How do you know that *suis* and *est* are to be found under *être*? Or that *a* and *as* are to be found under *avoir*? If you don't know the language well enough, you will need an exhaustive dictionary that will help you out. (Some dictionaries list irregular verb forms in a table at the back, and it is sometimes worth checking this if you suspect the word you are having trouble with is a past-tense form of a verb—such tables are often a useful resource.)

Many languages, including Malay and Indonesian, add prefixes and suffixes to words that change their meanings or add shades of meaning. These variations are only listed in the dictionary under the root word. You have to distinguish the prefix or suffix from the root word before you can look it up. Similarly, in Hebrew, conjunctions and prepositions are added to the root word.

Some software programs can help beginners facing this problem. The Transparent Language programs, for example, allow the user to click on any word in the text to find out what part of speech it is (that is, whether it is a noun, verb or adjective and so on), and to discover its root or 'dictionary form'. This can be extremely helpful in the early stages of learning a language when you don't recognise words.

As I mentioned earlier, if you are learning a language that uses ideographs, (Chinese is the most obvious example), you will need more than one kind of dictionary. You will need one that uses familiar roman characters at first, but eventually you will want to look up unfamiliar characters, whose sounds you do not know, and will have to buy yourself a dictionary in which characters are organised by pattern or by stroke count.

Don't be discouraged if it is difficult at first to find what you want using your dictionary. It is necessary to be patient at the beginning, and wait until you have built up some basic knowledge of a language. Suddenly, it will all start to make sense, and you will find what you are looking for much more easily. In the meantime, use other resources, including the grammar and vocabulary sections in your textbooks and native-speaker friends.

Recorded material

8

eight
οκτώ
huit
acht
ocho
восемь
delapan
kahdeksan

You need to listen to the language right from the beginning. Don't begin a written course before listening to the language. At the very least, you need a phrasebook with a recorded supplement. There are a number of inexpensive language programs for travellers available. Most good bookstores carry some. Check to see that the phrases given are relevant to your needs. A phrasebook with accompanying cassette or CD is an essential tool for learning your language.

Imitate the music of the language

As you listen to your recordings of the language, try to imitate the speaker as closely as possible. Sometimes you may feel foolish because the way the speaker says the phrases and sentences may sound strange to you. The intonations in each language are quite different. Copy the speaker's accent, pronunciation, and the changes in tone as closely as you can. Listen to the vowel sounds. The phonetic equivalents in your textbook may be close, but there will be subtle differences. Listen for them and try to imitate them as well as you can.

Use the pause button on your player frequently. Repeat each phrase and sentence after the speaker. Some recordings will have pauses in the recording to allow you to do this. Don't just be a passive listener—use the pauses to speak the language. I found that my first attempts to speak several languages left me tongue-tied. I had trouble forming words and sentences. Speaking aloud is the easy way to overcome this difficulty. Break the words up into syllables and speak them one syllable at a time, then two at a time, until you can put the words together. You need to be able to speak the language as well as be able to understand it.

As you speak, try to focus on the concept you want to communicate, rather than thinking through a word-for-word translation of what you might say in English. Try to speak directly in the language; try to think in the language. This is the only way to become fluent.

Complete language courses

There are many complete language courses with cassettes or CDs available. Should you buy one? If so, which one(s) should you buy? I definitely recommend that you buy one. You have the choice of Foreign Service Institute (FSI), Linguaphone, Assimil, Living Language, Transparent Language, Pimsleur and many others. Your choice will depend, to some extent, on your personality and how you learn. Each course has its pros and cons.

Generally, I would recommend your major audio language program should be recorded entirely in your target language. It will encourage you to think in the language and you will learn more in less time.

Courses that mix the target language with explanations in English are useful, but I would advise you to use them as secondary or supplementary tools. When you are driving, for example, you can follow new lessons more easily if they are explained in your own language. Recordings that are entirely in your target language can be played as well when you drive, but are only useful for revision.

Some language programs available in bookstores promise that you will learn the language in six weeks or four months. If they are cheap, there is no reason why they shouldn't be added to your tools. Any recorded material is useful in helping you understand the spoken word. However, learning from a language program always requires effort. Often the impression is given that if you just put the recording in your player and sit back, you will automatically learn the language—as though language learning were entirely passive, something that simply happens. Take it from me, that is nowhere near the truth. There are many language programs offered second-hand that have truly never been used. Sometimes advertisements state that 'only the first cassette has ever been played'.

Some audio programs present the learner with a list of drills— language-laboratory-type exercises in which you are given a sentence and asked to change one word in the sentence or to change the tense. Again, such programs can be used in addition to your major course, but I don't believe they should be your chief route to learning a language. I find such repetition boring, and it does not provide a very good return on my time. I try to avoid anything that looks like work because I assume I won't stick with it. In the following sections I will discuss some of the courses I find the most useful and more entertaining. I should note, though, that the final choice depends to a large degree on your personality. Some people enjoy exercises and drills and thrive on this kind of language learning. If this is your learning style, by all means use such materials or, at least, use them to support your other learning aids. Your tastes and preferences may be different to mine.

Assimil

Personally, I like the Assimil courses. I learnt to speak acceptable German in two months using only the Assimil course for twenty to thirty minutes a day. The entire course took around six months, plus some extra time to complete the 'second wave', studying the grammar. The courses are relatively inexpensive and are more effective than courses costing ten times as much, or more. I currently possess Assimil courses for French, German, Russian, Italian, Spanish, Polish, Dutch and Hebrew.

I like Assimil because the lessons are broken up into easy segments for each day's learning. (Although sometimes, towards the end of the course, I have taken two days to complete a lesson because I found the going tough.) Each lesson has a humorous cartoon to illustrate text from the day's lesson and a short exercise drill. You push the pace through the first half of the course, reading and listening to the lessons and following the explanations. You do not have to memorise anything or learn the grammar. All you do is read the text and the explanations and familiarise yourself with the words and the grammar. The next day, you move on to the next lesson, even if you have not learnt the previous lesson perfectly. You review the parts you are not sure of in the following lessons. I review the previous three or four lessons each day anyway, so I know I will pick up what I may have missed (or forgotten) from the previous lessons. Every so often I listen to the previous twenty or thirty lessons, and I find that I can easily understand them. When you are about a third to halfway through the course, you begin doing grammar and translation drills, beginning again with lesson one. You translate the English text back into the foreign language. This is now quite easy, because it is all old stuff by now—you have been working with and using the vocabulary for two months or more. This means your learning is way ahead of your drills and translation into the foreign language. You continue your way through the course doing a new lesson each day and reviewing an old one, about fifty lessons behind. By now you should be finding it easy. This is how you learnt your mother tongue. You learnt to say, 'I am hungry' and not to say, 'I is hungry'. Why didn't you say, 'I is hungry'? You didn't know the rules of grammar, but you knew it just didn't sound right. If you studied grammar at school, you learnt the rules you were already using unconsciously. This conscious learning is Assimil's second wave.

I also like the Assimil language courses because the text introduces you to native speakers of your target language. It is a friendly course, rather than just giving the learner sentences to use at the airport, at the hotel and so on. The speakers introduce you to the customs and culture of their country. You feel you get to know the people. Another reason that I like Assimil is that you get more vocabulary per CD or cassette than you do on recordings with drills, because the courses are recorded entirely in the language you are learning. I feel you get a better return for your time. It is much easier and more pleasant, too, to review old conversations and humorous stories than it is to review old drills. Ten minutes of reviewing your Assimil recordings will give you a far greater return on your time than ten minutes of reviewing a recording of drills with explanations in English.

The fact that Assimil audio materials are recorded entirely in the language is satisfying when I am replaying old lessons I have already completed, because I am listening to the language I am learning and also *thinking* in it—something you can't do if you are listening to explanations in English. My mind tunes itself to the language. In five or ten minutes, I can listen to the lessons for the past week and revise what I have learnt.

Transparent Language

The Transparent Language programs on CD-ROM are good, too. I have bought the complete Transparent Language programs for Swedish, Chinese, Hebrew, Spanish and Russian and would highly recommend them. They certainly teach the spoken language, including all the important phrases you need to know. Their major downside is that they only work on a computer and aren't good for learning on the go. However, you can copy the conversations onto a cassette tape or audio CD so that you can listen to them whenever you want, perhaps reviewing your lessons while driving your car or jogging. The audio section of a Transparent Language program is recorded entirely in the target language. Transparent Language allows you to play the sound at four different speeds, repeat a word as often as you like, and see a complete description and grammatical explanation of each word while you listen. It translates each phrase and gives the literal meaning as well. You can save the text of the recorded speech as a text or document file that you can print out to review and to work with by yourself.

Transparent Language's 101 Languages of the World program gives introductory lessons in seventy-six languages with extra information and vocabulary for twenty-five others. If you are not sure about learning a language, if you only want basic information, or if you just want to learn enough for a flying weekend-visit to the country, it is an excellent choice. Also, it may be the best program available for some of the more obscure languages. I suggest that you make the 101 Languages of the World program part of your learning material. I used the program to make my own survival course in Malay. I recorded the audio and printed the text, writing my translation along with it and bound it in a folder to use as my survival textbook. Transparent Language also offers free basic survival courses for a number of languages on its website.

In Australia, you can buy the Nodtronics Eureka language programs for less than ten dollars. Each disk contains the Transparent introductions to ten languages. I highly recommend this option, too.

Pimsleur

Many people swear by Pimsleur language programs. They are not my favourites, because they have no written text, they are too expensive, and they take too long to teach the language. You can learn a complete language on three or four CDs or cassette tapes with Assimil, but you have hardly begun with Pimsleur when you have completed your fourth tape or CD. The explanations are given in English and each lesson lasts thirty minutes. Thirty minutes is a long time to spend reviewing an old lesson.

On the other hand, Pimsleur takes you through the basics of the language and has you speaking the language in imaginary situations right from the beginning. Pimsleur is strong on drills and Assimil is not strong in that area. Also, the approach to the spoken language is different—Pimsleur has you speaking the language in context, rather than memorising and parroting words and phrases. For instance, the speaker will say, 'You have just met someone, how do you introduce yourself?' or 'You want to ask if the person speaks English. What do you say?'

Another benefit of Pimsleur is that when you are introduced to a new word that might be difficult to pronounce, the speaker introduces one syllable at a time and has you repeat the syllables and join them together until you can easily say the word.

I have bought 'Quick and Simple' introduction courses for several languages from Pimsleur. They are quite inexpensive when purchased from <www.amazon.com> and they will start you off in the language, but they give you no idea of how the language is written. Still, they may provide all you need for a lightning visit to the country. Also, it is like a 'try before you buy'. You can buy the introductory lessons cheaply and then, if you like them, buy the complete course. When it looked like I would be spending a lot of time in Asia I bought the Pimsleur Quick and Simple Chinese program and it served my purpose well.

You can find some sample Pimsleur language lessons online at <www.sybervision.com/freeaudio.htm>. This will allow you to listen to a full lesson in a number of languages. Try them and see what you think. The audio files are intended to be played over the internet, so the sound quality is nowhere near as good as the recorded courses you will buy, but they will still give you a good idea of what you are getting.

Other recorded material

Recorded music is a pleasant way to supplement your learning. Often you can find the lyrics to the songs on your CDs or tapes on the internet. Each time you sing a song you are revising the vocabulary. Children's songs are an easy choice. You can often buy recorded children's songs with an accompanying book with the lyrics. You can also seek out children's song books with words and music. Visit foreign-language bookshops in your capital city or community-language bookshops. They always have a stock of children's books and recordings.

As I have mentioned previously, you can watch movies with subtitles on television or buy or hire DVDs with subtitles. You can even watch the movie in your own language and read the subtitles in the foreign language. I bought movies in Singapore and Malaysia with the soundtrack in English and subtitles in Malay. This is a pleasant way to learn and revise your vocabulary. It is certainly not hard work.

When you buy DVDs, look at the back to see which language soundtracks they have. If you are learning an obscure language, DVDs with a soundtrack in your language may be difficult to find. Even if the DVD is in English with subtitles in your target language, it may still be well worthwhile. Use the pause button frequently to examine the foreign subtitles and make sense of them.

Children's stories

Listening to recorded children's stories is another pleasant option. The vocabulary should be easy and basic. You can download stories from the internet or buy them from foreign-language bookshops. Visit a foreign-language bookshop and look for children's books with accompanying cassettes or CDs.

Audio books

There is a good choice of audio books recorded in languages other than English. Do an internet search for 'audio books' in the language you are learning. You can telephone local community-language or foreign-language bookshops to ask what they have. Audio books are a great way to tune your ear to the language and to get used to understanding and even thinking in your target language. Buy a printed copy of the book as well so you can follow the text and check any words or passages you do not understand. You should also obtain a copy of the book in English, if possible, so you can see how the idioms are translated.

Internet

You can often download talks and spoken material from the internet. At first, if you don't understand these materials, they will be of limited use at best, unless you are able to download a transcript of the talk as well. Then you can easily check the meanings of words and phrases you don't understand. This option will become more useful as you improve your skills.

You can listen to online radio stations around the world — the sound quality is quite good. Sometimes a radio station will offer news broadcasts in simple language with a printed text so you can follow what the newsreaders are saying. Finding an appropriate station is not difficult: if you were learning Icelandic, for example you could do a search for 'learn Icelandic language'. Searching on Google using these words produces just fewer than half a million results. I have searched for 'Iceland radio stations' and been surprised by the response. The information is out there. Once you have found the right sites, you can listen to your target language while you work on your computer.

You can also use the internet to search for books, videos and DVDs in the language you are learning. There is an abundance of recorded and spoken material available if you look for it. Make use of it. Recorded material not only teaches you the correct pronunciation for the language but also enables you to tune your brain to the language.

Vocabulary

nine
εννέα
neuf
neun
nueve
девять
sembilan
yhdeksän

Most of the effort in learning another language is mastering the vocabulary. Grammar will often take care of itself. Although grammar is important and necessary, it is not usually the problem when you can't understand what you need to know—it is almost always vocabulary.

If you have a large vocabulary, you can usually understand what you read or hear and you can usually make yourself understood. This chapter is devoted to learning vocabulary as quickly and easily as possible.

You will find there are several ways of saying most things in any language. You can choose to express yourself in the way you find easiest, using the vocabulary you know. The problem is, not everyone has read your language textbooks; others will use different words to say things to you, so the bigger your vocabulary, the easier it will be to communicate.

When I learnt German I could speak to be understood, because I was in charge of the vocabulary I used, but when others answered me I couldn't control how they expressed themselves. I couldn't control the words they chose. A single word or turn of phrase sometimes threw me. For example, when I applied for a position with the international electronics firm in Germany I talked about earlier, one of the first questions I was asked was, '*Was für ein Landsman sind Sie?*' The interviewer was asking what my nationality was, but I hadn't heard this question expressed in quite this way before (literally, 'What for a countryman are you?') and I had to say I didn't understand him. He wasn't impressed, but I persuaded the company to hire me anyway. That was the position where my first task was to translate a technical text from English to German.

Of course, there are strategies you can use to get around such difficulties. You can always ask people with whom you are speaking to say something again a different way. Often, though, instead of using different words, they will just say the same thing again, more slowly and louder. This is not much help. When this happens, you could try paraphrasing what you *think* they are saying, and then ask, 'Is this what you are telling me? Are you telling me this?' Ask them questions to encourage them to say what they mean in different words.

Most words in the language you are studying will be learnt in context. If you are learning medical words, they will be repeated as you study your subject. The same applies to any other subject, whether it be religion, politics, physics or football. You will constantly be reminded of words you need to know and you will learn them naturally and easily. If you are confronted by a word on a daily basis you will soon find that you recognise it without any special effort. This is how you learnt your own language. You didn't do special drills to master vocabulary — daily reminders through natural usage were all that was necessary. This is how you will learn most words in your new language. It is easy, automatic, and stress-free.

However, to build on the vocabulary you will acquire effortlessly, I am going to show you another easy way to master a huge vocabulary in record time.

The fast way to a huge vocabulary

Some years ago I signed up for some Russian language lessons in the city of Melbourne. A student who wanted to work her way through university gave me one-on-one tuition at a private language school.

She had a set textbook (which I didn't like) and we would work through a lesson each week. I used the opportunity to ask questions from the course I was studying at home and to get help with my pronunciation. We got on well for some months, and then she began to give me a difficult vocabulary list to learn each week in preparation for my next lesson. To learn the new words, I used the methods I had devised myself (which I will teach you in this chapter). My attitude was, 'Why do today what you can put off doing until tomorrow?' Often I would leave it until the last minute, travel to the city, and drink a cup of coffee in a coffee shop while I memorised the entire vocabulary for the lesson.

In class, my instructor would quiz me and I would answer correctly.

Finally she told me that she had never had a student last for so long. She hadn't known how to take me any further with the language, so she had done with me what she had done with all of her previous students. When she had nothing more to teach, she would give an impossible vocabulary assignment, and the student would quit. In my case it hadn't worked, so she asked me if I would simply tell her college employer that I had learnt what I wanted and then finish up. She was worried her employer would realise that she wasn't capable.

The only way I was able to memorise the vocabulary each week was by using the method I am about to teach you. My contention is that if the method I am about to teach you works for Russian, it will work for any language. And indeed it does. A man studying Japanese once asked me to give him a private lesson and teach him how to memorise a Japanese vocabulary, even though I spoke no Japanese. I worked with him for about an hour and a half and we memorised around 150 Japanese words. He left satisfied he had learnt a valuable basic vocabulary. I was pleased that I had learnt them as well, and I had to decide for myself if I wanted to use what I had learnt and begin studying Japanese. I decided I didn't want to learn Japanese at that time, so I lost it all. I will show you how to use my method to put information into your short-term memory, and then easily transfer it to your long-term memory. The method is easy and fun.

Firstly, I tell myself that there is no panic to learn the vocabulary. That saves me from worrying if I will remember the words when I need them. I know the knowledge will come with time. That gives me the right mental attitude to start learning. My first concern is to recognise words in the foreign language and also to recognise the grammar. I don't worry about learning the rules. That will come later. I am continually in my first wave (passive stage) of learning the language so far as new material is concerned. By the time I reach the second wave, or active stage, I am confident the vocabulary will be there when I need it because of repetition.

If I want to learn the words quickly, so that I can use them immediately if I need them, I tell myself that I will be in control of how I learn my vocabulary. I call this 'active learning' as opposed to passive learning.

In the next section, I will tell you how I do this.

Active learning

The first step in active learning is hearing or reading the word I have to learn. If the word has no clear connection with its English equivalent I ask myself, 'What word or words does it *sound like* in my language?' This forces me to concentrate on the foreign word. I try to think of a word that it sounds like. Sometimes the English word I think of doesn't sound very much like the target language word at all, but it is as good as I can do. Maybe only one syllable sounds like a familiar word. No problem. It doesn't have to sound exactly like the word, but only something *like* it—enough to remind me of the word.

Then I make a mental picture of the sound-alike word and join it to the meaning with a crazy picture. Making the mental picture forces a high degree of concentration. You can't picture something without thinking about it. And, if you think of something else, the picture disappears. So, while you are making your mental picture, your concentration is total.

That is it. I don't have to remember the picture for the rest of my life, so there is no stress. I only have to remember the picture for five minutes or so until I review what I have learnt. The review reinforces the information in my mind and makes it even easier to remember the next time.

The crazier the picture, the more concentration it requires, the easier it is to remember and the more fun you have. You can entertain yourself with the crazy pictures you make.

There is a saying in Europe among people who learn languages that you have to learn a word and forget it seven times until you have really learnt it. My way, you learn a word just once. Not only that; the word goes immediately into your active vocabulary. Usually, when you learn a language, the new words go into your passive vocabulary first. That means you recognise the word when you hear it or see it. However, if you can translate from your own language to the foreign language, the word must have become part of your active vocabulary. It is much easier to translate from the foreign language to your own than the other way around. That is because our passive vocabulary is much larger than our active, but using my method, the words go straight into your active vocabulary.

Let's try some examples.

French

Let's say we are learning French and we learn that the French word for 'pig' is *cochon*, pronounced 'koshON'. (French has the stress on the final syllable. We show the stressed syllable by writing it in upper case letters.) How do we remember that the French word, *cochon*, means 'pig' in English?

Firstly, we ask ourselves, what English word sounds like *cochon*? We decide on the word 'cushion'. Cushion sounds like *cochon* so it represents the French word, *cochon*.

Next we join cushion to the meaning in English, 'pig'. Picture using **pigs** as **cushions** in your lounge room. You ask your guest to pull up a pig (cushion) and take a seat. When I say, 'Picture it', I actually mean that you should make a mental picture. See it in your mind. See the small pigs on your chairs instead of cushions. This forces high concentration and will enable you to remember the image when you need it.

We are not finished yet. We have to review the word ten minutes from now. Let's learn some more in the meantime.

The French for milk is *lait*, pronounced 'lay'.

'Lay' is of course an English word, so we simply take its meaning. We join 'lay' to milk. Picture a cow **lay**ing bottles or cartons of **milk**. That will do the job. See it in your mind. Don't just agree with the picture; actually see it.

Now we can go on to the next word.

Dormir means 'to sleep'. *Dormir* is pronounced 'doorMERE'. This is easy to remember, because we sleep in a dormitory. Dormitory is an English word which has its origin in the French verb. Picture yourself **sleep**ing in a huge **dorm**itory to force yourself to remember it. The job is done.

Grenouille means frog. The word is pronounced 'grenuhWEEyuh'. It sounds a bit like 'green wheel'. (Remember, the memory aid we choose doesn't have to sound exactly like the target language word, just close enough to remind you of it when you need it.) Picture a **frog** with no legs. The legs have been eaten, so the frog has been fitted with **green wheels** to get around. I hear the Beach Boys singing 'I Get Around' in the background as I imagine this.

Now, without looking back at the text:

- What is the French word for 'pig'?

- What is the French word for 'milk'?

- What is the French word for 'sleep'?

- What is the French word for 'frog'?

Are you impressed? Not only did you remember the words, but you remembered them from your active vocabulary — that is, you translated from your language to the foreign language.

Even if you missed one or two words, there is no need to worry — you will remember them at the next step. Simply picture the connection again in even more detail than before and then call it back correctly at your next review. Do it now. Using this method, your 'failures' will be better than most other language learners' successes.

Now the words are in your short-term memory. How do you transfer the words to your long-term memory? All you need to do is review the list and pictures each day for a week. Also, you should be using the words as you speak and study the language. The review should be automatic. Every time you read through your lessons, listen to your recorded lessons or use the language, you are working towards putting the information in your permanent memory.

Why do I call this active learning as opposed to passive learning? When you learn passively, you just read and listen to the new words and hope they will stick in your mind by themselves, usually by means of much repetition. When you learn actively, you determine how the words are learnt by making your own crazy pictures. You are in control. You decide the way you learn.

What if it doesn't work?

I had a student tell me, upset, that this method simply hadn't worked for him. He was doing something wrong, he said. The method was no good.

'What happened?' I asked.

'I tried to learn twenty words. I was showing off to my family. When I called them back, I had forgotten three of the words. What did I do wrong?'

I was amazed. I said, 'You forgot three words out of twenty. Look at it this way: you remembered seventeen words out of twenty. That's great. How many words would you have remembered without using the system?'

'I wouldn't have even tried it,' he said. 'My memory is hopeless.'

'Well your failure is much better than everyone else's success,' I told him. 'And it is much better than what you were doing before. What are you complaining about? Tell me, after you found out the three words you missed, did you remember them?'

'Yes, I was so embarrassed, I couldn't forget them.'

'So, you could call out all twenty words? So you remembered seventeen words out of the twenty, the first time you learnt them, and you learnt the other three words by revising them once more? That is fantastic success.'

'Yes, but what did I do wrong that I didn't learn them properly the first time?' he wanted to know.

My answer was that you make the sound-alike word in your own language as close as possible to the word you are learning in the foreign language. Then you make the connection as crazy as possible. That increases your level of concentration. It forces you to concentrate. Next you must see the picture as clearly as possible and with as much detail as possible. Make the picture as weird as you can and involve action. *See* it all happening. That also forces a high level of concentration. You are almost certain to easily recall the word when you need it.

I also told my student that for me, studying a new language is not a contest. I just want to learn the words as easily as possible. Who cares if I have to review the words another time before they become a part of my long-term, or permanent, memory? The end result is exactly the same. It is still much easier than repeating a word endlessly until it sticks by itself—and much more pleasant.

Now, let's try another language.

German

The German word for 'table' is *Tisch*, pronounced 'tish'. It sounds like 'dish'. Picture a giant **dish** with legs. You are using it for your breakfast **table**. When you prepare a meal you have to set the dish. Make the picture now. Actually see it in your mind.

When you saw it, you were using an extremely high level of concentration. When you make your own pictures and connections, rather than following my suggestions, you will be forced to think about the word and its meaning, and the technique will work even better.

What if you can't think of any sound-alike word? Firstly, the word doesn't have to be an exact, or even a very close, sound-alike. Even one syllable will do. But let's say you can't even come up with one syllable. In struggling to find a suitable sound-alike word, you have thought about the target language word with greater concentration than you normally would, so chances are you will still remember it. You win either way.

The word for 'treasure' is *Schatz* in German. It is pronounced like the English word 'shuts'. If you picture a pirate putting his **treasure** in a locked room, you will find it easy to remember. He **shuts** the door and locks it. The door shuts on the treasure. See the door of a safe or strongroom shutting on the treasure. You have it memorised.

The word *bleiben* means 'to remain'. The *ei* is pronounced like the *igh* in the English word 'high'. The short form of the word is *bleib*. *Bleib* (rhymes with 'vibe') sounds more or less like 'blob'. My own way to remember this verb was to recall a time when I had a ballpoint pen in my shirt pocket and it leaked, making a mess of my shirt. Although I tried, I couldn't remove the **blob**. It **remain**ed on my shirt. That is my connection between 'remain' and *bleib*. Now, make a picture for yourself. Visualise it carefully.

The German word for 'sick' is *krank*, which is pronounced much like the English word 'crank'. I would remember this by telling myself, 'Kids get **crank**y when they are **sick**'.

Russian

The Russian word for 'book' is *kniga*. (The *k* is pronounced, not silent.) The word is pronounced 'kuhNEEga'. Picture resting a

book (a Russian book) on your **knee** to read it, but pronounce the word 'knee' with the *k* sounded.

The Russian word for 'fast' is *bistro*. This is the origin of the English word 'bistro'—a place serving fast food. The Russian word is pronounced 'BEEstra'. Picture getting very **fast** food from a **bistro** and you have an easy connection.

The Russian word for 'read' is *chitayet*, pronounced 'chitAHyet'. (This is the third person singular form, used with 'she', 'he', or 'it'.) It sounds a little like 'Gee, tired'. Imagine that reading makes you tired. Picture yourself sleeping, with a book or newspaper on your lap. The connection is not with the book but with the thought, '**Gee**, reading makes me **tired**'.

The Russian word for 'house' is *dom,* pronounced like the English word 'dorm'. This will be easy to remember if you imagine using your **house** as a **dorm**.

Let's try another test.

- What is German for 'table'?

- What is Russian for 'fast'?

- What is German for 'sick'?

- What is Russian for 'book'?

- What is German for 'remain'?

- What is Russian for 'read'?

- What is German for 'treasure'?

- What is Russian for 'house'?

Did you get them all? Now, once more:

- What is the French word for 'pig'?

- What is the French word for 'milk'?

- What is the French word for 'sleep'?

- What is the French word for 'frog'?

All of these words are now in your active vocabulary. That is truly amazing. You are learning the words without even knowing it.

At training programs and lectures I have had people call out, 'Yes, but that won't work for Asian languages.' I know that this method works for any language, so I challenge them, 'Give me some words and we will learn them.'

Here are some words I have been given as a challenge.

Japanese

The Japanese word for 'apple' is *ringo*. Let's use the method you have just learnt. What does *ringo* sound like? How about 'ring', or 'ring go'?

Picture an apple growing on an apple tree. You put a **ring** over the **apple** and it is a tight fit. What happens as the apple continues to grow? Will the apple just expand above and below the ring or will the ring cut through the apple? Whatever your answer, if you picture the ring going over the apple, you will remember that *ringo* means 'apple' in Japanese.

The person who gave me the last example said that it was too easy; how about this one? The Japanese word for the verb 'to pour over oneself' or 'to bathe in' is *abiru*.

I chose to picture myself on top of Westminster **Abbey**. That gave me the first part of the word. Then I pictured **pouring** a sauce—a **roux**—over my head, so that it poured over the building and into the street (I already knew that *rue* is the French word for street). I had successfully joined the word to the meaning: *abiru* means 'to pour'.

Indonesian and Malay

Let's try Indonesian and Malay—two languages which share many words.

The word *pelajaran*, pronounced 'pelaJARan', means 'lesson' in both Indonesian and Malay.

Imagine that you have a **jar** of **ants** (jaran) for the teacher, because the teacher is your **pal** (pel). Picture yourself bringing the jar of ants to your **lesson**—your language lesson. My sound-alike elements may not be a great fit, but this picture has worked for me. It only has to stay in your memory for five or ten minutes until the first review. Then, as you review the word and its meaning, it will soon become part of your permanent memory.

Hendak, pronounced 'henDUCK', is the Indonesian/Malay word for 'to want' or 'to wish'. What do you **want**? What do you **wish** for? A **hen** and a **duck**. That is what you want to be happy. Already, you have the word memorised.

Suka, pronounced 'SOOka', is the Indonesian/Malay word for 'to like'. I would remember this by telling myself, 'I **like sugar**'. The word for 'sugar' is actually pronounced just like *suka* in several languages. That should be enough to remind you that the Malay word *suka* means 'to like'.

Keju, pronounced 'KAYjoo', is 'cheese' in Indonesian/Malay. Imagine a **cheese** so well-fermented that it is alive, and must be kept in a **cage**. That will remind you that *keju* is cheese.

Sejuk, pronounced 'SAYjook', is 'cold' in Indonesian/Malay. 'Chook' is an Australian word for 'chicken', so I think of (and picture) a frozen chicken, or **chook**. It is obviously **cold**—I can **see** it. This helps me remember that *sejuk* ('see chook') means cold in Malay. If 'chook' sounds too foreign to you, you might note that *sejuk* also sounds like 'say joke'. Picture yourself telling a **joke** that is in bad taste and meeting with a very **cold** reception. Alternatively, you could imagine yourself telling a joke you know about snow or a cold climate. The possibilities are endless. They are only limited by your imagination.

Panas, pronounced 'panUS', is 'hot' in Indonesian/Malay. If someone put **us** in a **pan** and put it on the stove, we would get **hot**. This will help you to remember that *panas* is 'hot'.

Has the method worked for the Asian languages?

- What is Japanese for 'apple'?

- What is Japanese for the verb 'to pour over oneself'?

- What is Indonesian/Malay for 'lesson'?

- What is Indonesian/Malay for the verb 'to wish'?

- What is Indonesian/Malay for the verb 'to like'?

- What is Indonesian/Malay for 'cheese'?

- What is Indonesian/Malay for 'cold'?

- What is Indonesian/Malay for 'hot'?

Aren't you amazed? You should be. This is the fast, easy way to learn a vocabulary in a foreign language. Can you see that you can not only memorise a vocabulary in record time, but also that you can have fun while you do it?

Hints to help you make mental pictures

Here are some rules to follow to help you make mental pictures and connections that will work:

1. **Exaggerate the size of objects you imagine.** Make them huge. This will make your mental picture memorable.

2. **Exaggerate numbers.** See millions of the objects you are picturing, not just one.

3. **Incorporate action**. Bring movement into the picture. See the connection actually happening.

4. **Substitute one object for another.** Substitute the meaning for the sound-alike and vice versa. For instance, we substituted 'pig' (*cochon*) for 'cushion' and sat on pigs instead of cushions. You could have substituted the other way and pictured keeping cushions in a cushion sty, trying to fatten the cushions for sale. You would have pictured the cushions wallowing in the mud and fighting each other for their food.

5. **Make the picture ridiculous.** We remember the absurd and we are inclined to forget the ordinary. Making the picture ridiculous makes it memorable.

6. **Making the picture risqué can help you remember it.** You don't have to explain to anyone else how you were able to memorise the vocabulary.

7. **Actually *see* the picture.** Sometimes, people will think of a brilliant connection and then neglect to actually see the mental picture. Making the picture in your mind will force a high level of concentration.

8. If inspiration fails you and you are unable to make a brilliant, ridiculous connection, **make an ordinary connection but then make sure you see the picture in your mind with as much detail as possible**. See it as clearly as you can.

Following these rules will allow you to memorise the greatest number of words in the least possible time with the minimum effort.

You can rule up columns in a notebook and fill out your vocabulary as demonstrated in the following examples. Read over these examples to reinforce the new words you have just learnt.

French

Word	Pronounced	Meaning	Sounds like	Picture
cochon	koshON	pig	cushion	use a **pig** as a **cushion**
lait	lay	milk	lay	a cow **lay**s **milk**
dormir	doorMERE	to sleep	dorm	we **sleep** in the **dorm**
grenouille	grenuhWEEyuh	frog	green wheel	a **frog** with **green wheels**

German

Word	Pronounced	Meaning	Sounds like	Picture
Tisch	tish	table	dish	use a giant **dish** as a **table**
Schatz	shuts	treasure	shuts	a pirate **shuts treasure** in a locked room
bleib	blibe	remain	blob	**blob** (stain) **remain**s, I can't remove it
krank	crahnk	sick	crank	kids get **crank**y when they are **sick**

Russian

Word	Pronounced	Meaning	Sounds like	Picture
kniga	kuhNEEga	book	knee	I rest my **book** on my **knee** to read
bistro	BEEstra	fast	bistro	**fast** food at **bistro**
chitayet	chitAHyet	read	gee, tired	**gee**, **read**ing makes me **tired**
dom	dawm	house	dorm	we use our **house** as a **dorm**

Japanese

Word	Pronounced	Meaning	Sounds like	Picture
ringo	ringo	apple	ring go	**ring go**es over **apple**
abiru	abiru	to pour over oneself	abbey roux	**pour** a **roux** on myself at Westminster **Abbey**

Indonesian/Malay

Word	Pronounced	Meaning	Sounds like	Picture
pelajaran	pelaJARan	lesson	pal, jar, ant	teacher is your **pal**, give a **jar** of **ants** in your **lesson**
hendak	henDUCK	to wish	hen duck	I **wish** I had a **hen** and a **duck**
suka	SOOka	like	sugar	I **like sugar**
keju	KAYjoo	cheese	cage	**cheese** kept in a **cage**
sejuk	SAYjook	cold	see chook	I **see** a frozen (cold) **chook**
panas	panUS	hot	pan, us	if someone puts **us** in a **pan** we will be **hot**

Let us look at what you have just done. You have memorised the meanings of twenty words that you can translate either way; that is, from English to the foreign language or from the foreign language to English. That means the words are part of your active vocabulary. How long did it take you to learn them? It depends on how quickly you read the preceding section. It may have taken you between ten and twenty minutes. Let's take twenty minutes as our estimate. You learnt the words at the rate of about one word a minute. That is a great return on your time. Actually, it is quite easy to memorise words using this method at two words per minute, and it is quite possible that you have just done so. Learning a foreign vocabulary has never been easier.

After trying this method, one of my students said, 'You are learning the words without even trying to or, without even knowing you have learnt them.'

I remember sitting with a private student once and thinking that as I was feeling tired that evening, I would let him 'see' the mental pictures alone—I wouldn't make the effort myself this time. (I usually learn everything with my students as part of my method.) After the student learnt his vocabulary, I discovered that I could call out all of the words and their meanings as well. I had learnt the words without trying to do so, without even knowing that I had.

Please note that when you are writing words in your vocabulary notebook to memorise you should be taking them from a meaningful context: they should be used in your texts, or perhaps come from a phrase that is important to you. Don't just take words at random from a dictionary to learn unless they are strategic, high-frequency words, or technical terms you need to know.

Learning the gender of a new word

In many languages you will find that nouns have gender; that is, they are either masculine or feminine, or even neuter. For example, 'window' might be feminine, 'glove' might be masculine and 'letter' might be neuter. There is generally no clear reason for the choice—it just has to be learnt. Often the word ending will tell you if the word is masculine, feminine or neuter, but there are always exceptions.

There are some ways to learn the gender with the word. When you make your mental picture, you could include men or women in it, so that you will not only remember the word and its meaning, but also the gender. Or you could picture the feminine words wearing dresses or skirts and the masculine words wearing trousers or doing something you consider masculine or manly. (I will look at gender in further detail in chapter 15, which deals with grammar.)

Other ways to learn vocabulary

There are many other ways to learn vocabulary. Often, textbooks will give you a connection between the foreign word and the word you are learning. You could use their suggestions — or use them in addition to the crazy picture method. Look out for common derivations or similarities between English words and words in your target language, too, as these are often very helpful.

Use derivations to help you learn

There are many words in other languages that have a similar derivation to their English equivalent, and many English words are derived from foreign words. These target language words can be learnt by just noting the derivation. Better still, you can combine the methods.

If you were learning Malay or Indonesian, you would learn that the word for 'person' is *orang*. This is where we get the name of the ape, 'orang-utan'. *Orang-utan* in Malay means 'man of the forest'.

Many English words derive from French. Read any French text and you will find many familiar words. Watch out, though, for 'false friends' — words that look similar but have different meanings. For instance, the French verb *demander* does not mean 'to demand', but rather, 'to ask'.

When my daughter was sick in Germany, the doctor told us to 'kontrollieren' her temperature. I asked him, 'How do we control it?' He explained that we had to *monitor* her temperature — there was no control involved. The German verb *kontrollieren* means to monitor or to check, rather than control. These are the kinds of misunderstandings that can start wars. There is a big difference between, 'We want to monitor the border' and 'We want to control the border.' So, be careful of words that look and sound similar to English but have a different meaning, or a different shade of meaning.

Identifying patterns and similarities

English is classified as a Germanic language, and if you know one it is easy to learn the other. The German word for 'knee' is *Knie* (with the *k* pronounced). German for 'house' is *Haus*, which is pronounced just like the English word. We have already learnt that *krank* means 'sick', so it makes sense that 'hospital' is *Krankenhaus*, literally a 'sickhouse' or house for the sick. These are easy words to learn. 'Night' is *Nacht* and 'knight' is *Knecht*. *Schreiben* means 'to write'—this is the derivation of the English word 'scribe'. *Arm* means 'arm' (as well as 'poor'), *Hand* means 'hand' and *Finger* means finger. *Fuss* means 'foot', so *Fussball*, of course, means 'football'.

Ch in German often corresponds with *gh* in English. *Lachen* is 'laugh'; *Recht* is 'right'; *Macht* is 'might' (meaning power or strength) and, as we have seen, *Knecht* is 'knight' and *Nacht* is 'night'. These words are easily learnt.

If you also remember that *v* in German often corresponds with *f* in English and that a German double *s* corresponds with *t* in English, the meanings of many German words will suggest themselves. *Vergessen* means 'to forget'; *Strasse* means 'street'; *beissen* means 'to bite'; *hassen* means 'to hate'. Treat these words as gifts. There is no effort involved in remembering them.

You can instantly learn many words in Spanish. For instance, the ending *-ity* in English usually corresponds with *-idad* in Spanish. *Universidad* means 'university', *eternidad* is 'eternity' and *velocidad* means 'velocity'. The ending *-ist* in English corresponds with *-ista* in Spanish. The word 'artist' becomes *artista*, 'list' becomes *lista*, 'racist' becomes *racista*, and of course, 'linguist' becomes *lingüista*. Many words ending in *-ic* in English are the same in Spanish, but with an *o* added to the end. 'Comic' becomes *comico*, 'academic' becomes *académico*, 'elastic' and 'electric' become *elástico* and *eléctrico*. You can recognise these words at a glance. Make use of these words. They have been given to you for free, as a gift.

★ ★ ★

If you know 1000 of the most common words in your target language then you should be able to speak the language quite well. (There are many words in English that you know and recognise but have never spoken.) The most common 1000 words make up between 80 and 90 per cent of normal speech. You can certainly achieve a basic vocabulary of 1000 words in your target language within two weeks. When you have a basic vocabulary, it is not difficult to pick up the other words you need. You have a foundation to build on. You can get by superbly well in a language with the most common 3000 words—and learning 3000 words is not an impossible task.

Learning a language is more than vocabulary

People sometimes tell me that there is much more to learning a language than learning the vocabulary. This is true. There is no argument about that. Their point seems to be, though, that I am teaching others how to learn vocabulary quickly and that vocabulary alone is not enough to allow them to learn the language. Rejecting my vocabulary learning techniques for this reason is like telling a footballer not to practise kicking the ball because football is more than just accurate kicking. Accurate kicking is an essential skill—just like vocabulary building. Students *need* to know as many words in their chosen language as possible. I am obviously not telling language learners to drop the study of grammar and sentence construction and all of the other skills they need. What I am saying is that learning a vocabulary is important: *here is an easy way to do it*. Learning the vocabulary of our target language is part of our adventure — it is not an unwelcome chore.

Recent research has shown that when we learn a second language our brain develops a speech centre for that language. With each successive language we learn, we develop new speech centres in our brain. It has been shown that these speech centres are independent of each other and have no physical connection to our memory.

As you memorise words in your new language, they are firstly stored in your short-term memory, then in your long-term memory and, with use, they become part of your speech centre. Because there is no physical connection between your memory and your speech centre, many people connected with language learning oppose memorising foreign vocabularies. I am not convinced. The new words you learn by memorisation become part of your knowledge of the new language with use and are there in your speech centre to use when you need them.

Combine the main method of learning vocabulary we have just learnt with the passive and active method of soaking up the language and you will find it can only help. It will certainly speed up the process. I say, use any method you can that helps you reach your goal.

Your plan

ten
δέκα
dix
zehn
diez
десять
sepuluh
kymmenen

In this chapter, we will put together a language-learning plan, and then put it into operation. Before we start discussing what you will do day by day and week by week, though, I would like to make a few general suggestions.

Firstly, it is important to have some kind of schedule. Try to stick to it.

If you have a recorded language course, include one lesson each day, or part of a lesson, depending on how much information is introduced each lesson. Play the recording of the full lesson each day, even if it takes several days or a week to complete the lesson. This also applies to computer-based language courses.

As a general rule I would say, do a little every day, and a lot some days. Immerse yourself completely in the language from time to time.

My suggested plan should help you to learn your language as well as possible in the shortest possible time. You can modify it in any way you wish—you are in control. You might like to make further modifications to the plan as your circumstances change or as you pick up new material.

It might be a good idea to write your own plan in the front of your first language notebook or pin it on the wall in the place where you will do your study. You can change your plan as often as you like. Nothing is written in concrete—remember, you are your own teacher and you make the decisions.

Slowly but surely or quickly but poorly?

For many of my learning strategies I teach a 'quickly-but-poorly' approach. Many people react very strongly against this—it goes against everything they have ever been taught. They feel they have to master the current lesson perfectly before moving on to the next. The 'quickly-but-poorly' brigade just read and listen to the lesson, note the meanings of words and grammar explanations and then move on without worrying if they have perfectly mastered the material or not. They know they will grasp the information fully in the coming days and weeks as they revise the material each day. This takes the stress and hard work out of learning. Students who take the quickly-but-poorly approach progress much more quickly than the slowly-but-surely people. They might only retain 80 per cent of what they learn, but their 80 per cent is probably double or triple the amount the slowly-but-surely people achieve. If you adopt this approach, you will be more highly motivated, as you see tangible results for your efforts and if you are not so critical of your so-called failures.

So, work your way through each day's lesson. Note the meanings of the words and read the grammatical explanations without worrying about memorising them. You are only concerned about recognising the material during the 'first wave' or passive stage of your language study. You will review your lessons regularly anyway as your first wave of study continues; then you will actively consolidate the material in the second wave or active part of your study. By the time you reach the second stage, the vocabulary and grammar you have covered in the first wave should all seem easy and familiar to you when you come back to it.

First day

On the first day we become acquainted with the language. Here is a suggested outline of how you can do this:

1. Introduce yourself to the written language and rules of pronunciation.

2. Read the first few chapters of each textbook. (If you found it difficult to learn the rules of pronunciation, one chapter may be sufficient.) Don't worry about remembering it all. Read the explanations. Make notes in your working notebook. Write the important new words in your vocabulary notebook. Do any exercises mentally—just sufficient to see that you understand.

3. Read your phrasebook and look for phrases that are important to you—'hello', 'goodbye', 'please', 'thank you', 'excuse me', and so on—and write them in your own phrases notebook. Say the words and phrases out loud so they roll easily off your tongue.

4. Listen to your language tape or CD. Follow the pronunciation. If you have a dual cassette recorder you might like to edit your important phrases so that you can play them in the order you choose.

Second day

On the second day:

1. Revise your first day's effort.

2. Read the next lesson in each book. Again, don't worry about remembering it all just yet. All you want is to push ahead at a good pace. You will consolidate what you learn as you go.

3. Read through your phrasebook and find and write new phrases—perhaps 'Where is?', 'Do you have …?', 'Do you speak English?', 'How much?', 'I would like …', 'I need' or similar. Say them out loud.

4. Listen to your tape or CD program.

Don't forget to read your lessons from the textbook and phrases from the phrasebook *out loud*. Speaking the language is an important part of the learning process.

Third and fourth days

Now you have made your acquaintance with the language and have some idea of how it works, you can begin to learn the language in earnest. You don't have to commit it all to memory. You want to work in the beginning with high-frequency words, so that you will be reminded of them daily. A core vocabulary of 1000 words will get you a long way. The 1000 words you choose should be high-frequency words and words that are useful to you.

On the third and fourth days, you should:

1. Revise what you have already done.

2. Draw up a diagram of prepositions. (See page 31 in chapter 4 for an example.)

3. Work on a lesson in your textbooks.

4. Write down new phrases from your phrasebook.

5. Listen to your tape or CD.

6. Begin learning vocabulary. Select words from your phrasebook and textbooks.

7. Make your own sentences. Speak to yourself.

8. Begin writing your own survival course book.

Fifth and sixth days

1. Revise the previous day's work.

2. Make a chart of pronouns: 'I', 'you', 'she', 'he' and so on.

3. Tackle a new lesson from your textbooks or continue your lesson from yesterday.

4. Revise important phrases from your phrasebook.

5. Listen to your tape or CD.

6. Make your own sentences. Speak to yourself.

7. Continue to work on your survival course book.

Seventh day

Put day seven aside to revise the first week's work:

1. Read over what you have already learnt.

2.   Listen to your language tape and your language course.

3.   Listen to music and songs in the language.

4.   Read a joke book or jokes from the internet.

Writing the language

Learning a language not only involves reading, speaking and listening to the language, it also includes *writing* in the language. This last skill generally requires more effort than the other three, so many people are inclined to ignore this side of language learning. It is important that you are able to express yourself in writing. It is not as difficult as it may first appear. You just need to start. I was forced by circumstances to write letters in several European languages. I resisted the idea but I had no choice. When I got down to it, I discovered it wasn't so difficult.

You should start writing words and phrases in your notebook from the very beginning. This will help you to master the spelling of the language. Then, as you embark on your second or active wave of learning, you should start doing some written exercises. Write short notes to yourself as part of your everyday learning program. You have been speaking to yourself—now you will write to yourself in the language, too.

These days, when I have written a letter in a foreign language and I am not confident about it, I write it again in English and use the translation services offered by the Google or AltaVista websites to translate it. Then I check the new version against my original and see if I can make some improvements. I provide more information about these services and how to use them in chapter 18.

Week two

During week two, you should:

1. Revise what you have done in week one.

2. Make a chart or list of important verbs you have learnt.

3. Textbook lessons. Read them out loud.

4. Phrasebook—read out loud.

5. Listen to your tape or CD.

6. Translate simple headlines from an online newspaper or from material you have chosen from your textbook.

7. Learn vocabulary from your textbook or phrasebook.

8. Make your own sentences. Speak to yourself.

9. Learn from your survival course book. Read aloud and listen to your recording each day.

Begin each day's study with a quick revision of the previous day's lesson. Read earlier lessons just for fun. You will find they become incredibly easy after you have revised them a few times.

Write a list of words and phrases that are going to be important for you to know—technical words related to your profession, perhaps, or other words connected with your own personal reason for learning the language. Write them in a notebook and then write in the translation in your target language. Leave room for notes, because you might find you have to express some ideas quite differently in your target language.

You can take your time preparing and learning this list. You should add to it continually as you learn the language. Try to find literature that covers your own special interests and begin to work your way through it. Check out webpages on the subjects you would like to be able to discuss in your target language, too. Use these materials to discover both the words you need and the way the concepts are expressed.

Weeks three and four

In weeks three and four:

1. Revise what you have learnt in weeks one and two.

2. Continue doing lessons from your textbooks each day.

3. Read important phrases from your phrasebook out loud.

4. Write important vocabulary in your notebook and memorise them.

5. Listen to your tape or CD.

6. Translate jokes, riddles or online newspaper headlines.

7. Make your own sentences. Speak to yourself.

8. Learn from your survival course book. Read aloud. Listen to your recording.

9. Read newspaper headlines in your target language on the internet.

The 'active' stage of your study

By this time you will find you prefer one textbook above the others, or you might find the recorded language course the most useful. Make whichever tool you find most useful your main learning resource and use the others for support. Continue to read the explanations in several textbooks rather than just one. Your computer language course is unlikely to become your main method of learning, but you should still make good use of it.

At this point, you should also search on the internet for materials designed to help you achieve your goals. They are out there, so use them. Look for webpages in the language you are learning. Print out a page that doesn't look too difficult and work your way through it with a dictionary.

Continue to push the pace with your textbooks. Don't worry if you think you aren't remembering all of the vocabulary. You will pick it up with revision and will certainly master it when you come back to it during your second wave.

Week five or six

I recommend that you begin your second wave of grammar in week five or six, but you can of course leave it until later if you like—there is no hurry. Go back to lesson one in your textbooks and do the exercises. You should write down some examples, but you can do most of the exercises mentally. They should be easy by now.

During the fifth and sixth weeks, you should:

1. Begin the second wave of learning by going back to the first lessons in your textbooks and translating materials from English into your target language.

2. Continue learning new lessons from your textbook.

3. Plan an immersion day. (See chapter 16 for ideas on how to go about this.)

4. Keep adding words to your vocabulary notebook. Use the methods described in chapter 9 to memorise them.

5. Listen to old and new lessons on tape or CD.

6. Translate a webpage or comic.

7. Enrol in a class or meet speakers of your target language. (See chapters 13 and 14 for further information.)

8. Make your own sentences. Speak to yourself.

9. Learn from your survival course book.

10. Read newspaper headlines in your target language on the internet.

Now it is time to put together anything you can find and use all of the resources available to learn your language in the shortest possible time. Read children's books. Follow children's stories with recordings if you can find them. Comics are a good idea, too. They contain mainly spoken language, which is what you want at this stage. (Also, you won't become discouraged reading pages of dense text.) Watch movies in the language. Always read through the television guide to see when movies in your target language will be broadcast.

Work on pronunciation and sentence construction. These are what give you away as a foreigner. Practice repeating words and phrases from your language tapes. Ask friends who speak the language if you are pronouncing the words correctly.

Make good use of your major recorded course. Play the recordings often and tune your ear and your mind to the spoken language.

Push ahead daily with the program you have chosen as your main course. The rest of your material will be backup. Work with it.

Forge on ahead as quickly as you can and catch any grammar you miss when you come to the second wave.

The first step is to understand the language. The second step is thinking in the language and dreaming in the language. As you immerse yourself in the language, you will find you will start to dream in the language. This is the true (and the only) way to learn a language while you sleep. If you follow your plan and do a little everyday, this will happen sooner than you expect.

11 Using lost time

eleven
εντεκα
onze
elf
once
одиннадцать
sebelas
yksitoista

In study programs I conduct, I constantly tell my students to make use of 'lost' time. If you use lost time, you can put in more useful study time than your friends who are up studying half the night— and it will appear that you are doing next to no study at all.

What is lost time?

Lost time is the time you take to walk to the railway station or the bus stop. It is the time spent waiting in line at the bank or at the checkout at the supermarket. It is the time you are kept on hold on the telephone, or time spent sitting in a train, bus or plane. It is the time passed in a restaurant or cafe waiting for your order to arrive. All of us have lost time we can make use of.

This is time for revision. This is the time to bring out your notebook or flashcards. If you have your phrasebook or textbook with you, this time that would otherwise be lost can be put to good use.

There is other lost time as well. How about shaving, washing the dishes, ironing or doing routine jobs in the office or home? Any task that doesn't require concentration can fit in this category. These are ideal times for playing the recorded lessons and tuning your ear and brain to the spoken language. If you are unable to play your recordings while you are doing these jobs, at least you can talk to yourself in the language and put in some worthwhile practice.

You should always have recordings to play in your car while you are driving, too. You can concentrate on the road and the traffic at the same time. You can listen to the car radio in your own language without being distracted, so you should at least be able to have your language recording playing in the background while you drive without any trouble.

Taking time from other activities

When you use your lost time for revision, how much time are you taking from the activities you like to do? None at all. You are not taking time from other activities to study your language. You would be washing the dishes, ironing, shaving or driving anyway. This is time that would be otherwise lost and it is a huge bonus. You are effectively getting a lot of work done on your language without taking any time from other activities to do so. You are fitting more hours into your day. Whenever students tell me they haven't had time to apply my methods, I tell them they aren't using them correctly. Everyone has lost time they can put to use.

In my study seminars I teach students to use their lost time for specific tasks. Some tasks should be reserved for lost time: vocabulary or grammar revision are ideal. Always carry a set of flashcards and a textbook or joke book or other reading material in the language. While you are waiting in line at the bank or supermarket, get out your textbook or flashcards and do some revision. I always carry a book with me to read while I am waiting in line at the bank. It is not necessarily a language book; it can be any book that I am reading. I have always done so. People comment from time to time, but usually the comments are positive. I anticipate lost time and make sure I have reading material or language study aids with me. Otherwise I consider the time truly lost and I resent this waste. Sitting on public transport or on an aeroplane is torture for me if I don't have reading material. I always take both serious and light reading with me.

If you don't have anything to read in the checkout line in the supermarket, at least speak to yourself while you are waiting (not out loud, obviously) . See how many items there are in your trolley that you can name in your target language. Give yourself a running commentary on what you are doing or are going to do while you are waiting. It is all practice. It all helps.

Look at the magazines and newspapers at the checkout and see how much you can translate from English to your target language. You can certainly make better use of your time than just standing there and letting your brain sleep. All of this takes some effort and discipline at first. Make it a habit and you will find the effort isn't so great. You will begin to do it automatically. Making use of your lost time is like adding another year or two to your life.

Learning on the job

If you have colleagues at work who speak another language, you have a great opportunity to learn that language. If you have colleagues who speak the language you are learning, it is an extra bonus. If you work with native speakers of other languages, try to learn from them. You don't have to take time from your working hours. I have worked at several jobs where I could practise my new languages.

One of my colleagues, and a good friend, came from northern Africa and spoke a number of languages fluently. He used to speak with me in French on the job. Instead of asking a work-related question in English I would ask in French. He said I was the only person who was interested in speaking with him about where he lived and came from and about the languages he knew. You are very likely to find that there is someone at your workplace who would be delighted to cooperate in such a scheme. You can save up your questions about the language to ask your native speaker.

Use the time and opportunities you already have and you will learn your language at record speed as well as living a more fulfilled life.

Enjoy light reading

12
twelve
δώδεκα
douze
zwölf
doce
двенадцать
dua belas
kaksitoista

Learning a new language should be fun. You can minimise any stress by playing rather than working at the language. Light reading is an excellent way to do just this, so you should keep a good stock of fun reading material to hand. I like to read comics and joke books, fiction and non-fiction, newspapers, magazines and webpages in the language I am learning.

Comics

Comic books are an easy choice. Firstly, you can often guess the meaning from the pictures and the context. If you don't work out the meaning the first time, you may be able to guess at it the second or third time you come across the relevant words in the text. Secondly, you can often buy the same comic book in English (or your own native language), allowing you not only to check the meaning of unfamiliar words, but also to discover how the same concepts are expressed in the two different languages.

When I was learning French I used to buy *Le Journal de Mickey*—Mickey Mouse comics printed in France. The publishers of *Le Journal de Mickey* also produce books for children that can be fun to read. Because they are written for children the vocabulary is fairly simple and direct. They are available in almost any language.

I have copies of the *Junior Woodchucks' Manual* in French, Italian and German. They not only make interesting reading, but also offer an insight into the cultures and their differences. The French Junior Woodchuck manual has a different style and emphasis to the German version, and the Italian manual is different again. I also find the Tintin comic books to be both an enjoyable read and very useful in practising my target language. No-one should think any less of you if they see you reading Tintin in a different language while you are travelling by train or bus.

Jokes and joke books

Joke books which have single frame cartoons with a punchline are great when you feel too lazy to tackle a more difficult text. Short jokes and riddles are a good choice. A long text will discourage you, so tackle something short, snappy and entertaining. Collections of Peanuts comic strips are available in many languages. The effort required to read them is not too great, as you are just reading a few boxes with not much dialogue.

It is easy to find joke pages on the internet. Either find out the word for 'jokes' or 'cartoons' in the language you are learning and then search for it, or simply type in 'jokes' in English, but limit your search to websites and pages in your target language. (I explain how to do this in chapter 18.)

Books, magazines and newspapers

Look for books that you enjoy reading in English translated into your target language. At the very least, most foreign-language bookshops have the Harry Potter books in every language they carry. I have books by Agatha Christie in Russian as well as in English. I found them advertised on eBay. I read the Russian and English versions side by side with the help of a dictionary. This can be a pleasant means of learning the language.

Children's books are an excellent option. If you are worried about what others may think if you are caught reading children's literature, put a plain cover on the book so no-one knows what you are reading. Personally, I enjoy reading many books for children. The language in children's books is not too complicated. It is usually straightforward narrative and dialogue and will entertain you while you build your vocabulary and learn the idioms of the language.

You might like to subscribe to magazines in your target language, as well. At the beginning you will only need one magazine to work on, as you will have to look up most of the words in your dictionary and translating one paragraph will be a major effort. Your first magazine should last for months if you put it to good use. Translate the advertisements as well as the articles. Magazines for children are another good source of easy reading material, because articles are usually to the point and use common, useful words.

You should seek out material with easy vocabulary—words you already know or words whose meanings are easily recognised. Read about your hobbies or interests in your chosen language. Do you enjoy chess? Buy and read chess books and magazines in the language you are studying. I have read of chess masters who learned half a dozen languages, just so they could read international chess books and magazines. This sounds impressive, but it is no huge task. To follow the game notation, you only need to know the symbols for the pieces. You should also know the names of the pieces. Even if you want to read the notes on the games, the vocabulary used is limited. If you are interested in model aircraft, you will find magazines in your language of interest. If you follow a European football team, you are sure to find lots of reading material about them in your target language.

If you are interested in sports, you could choose any sporting team from the country whose language you are learning and read all about the team and its members. Look up the football, baseball and basketball results in the newspapers of the language. That will give you an added interest in the country and the language.

Reading materials on the internet

Whatever your interest, you will find something on the internet. You can use Google and other search engines to look for pages in the language of your choice. See chapter 18 for further information.

As I have noted elsewhere, you can read the headlines of newspapers in your target language on the internet. If an article interests you, you can print it and translate it at your leisure. You can download whole newspapers from the internet or just print out the articles that interest you. There are always the cartoons as well.

Search for online magazines that cater for your interests. As well as reading the newspaper headlines in your target language, find online magazines in your target language that deal with your special interests. Print out the pages that interest you and take them with you when you travel or to read in your coffee breaks.

All of the options I have discussed above add variety to your learning. Reading magazines, books and online materials is more interesting than just reading your textbooks. It is also a great way to practise your target language. It is easier to snatch a minute or two during the day to read a book or magazine than it is to find someone to speak with in the language you are learning. The more ways you find to attack your language learning, the better, and the greater your enjoyment.

Language classes

13

thirteen
δεκατρία
treize
dreizehn
trece
тринадцать
tiga belas
kolmetoista

An important option when you are studying a language on your own is to take a language class. Wait a moment—how can you be studying a language on your own if you are taking lessons?

If you are following the strategy I recommend, you are still studying alone, even when you are taking classes. You are using multiple textbooks; you are listening to the language and reading the language on your own. A language class is just another tool. It is especially useful if you don't have a native-speaker friend you can go to for help with the language when you need it. You are still your own main teacher and you can determine what you get from the lessons. You will attend classes *in addition* to your own work.

I wouldn't enrol in a class too early in your language study. You need to know what it is you need to learn to obtain the full benefit. As you study, you will naturally have more and more questions.

Formal lessons are a form of self-discipline

Taking a weekly lesson in your language forces you to maintain discipline. It is a useful strategy if you think you might not have the willpower to stick with the language. It is easier to work at the language if you have committed yourself to attending classes. The lessons give you an opportunity to ask questions and check what you have learnt. If you have to prepare for each lesson, this gives you a plan or structure for your study.

Getting the most out of your language class

To get the most from your lessons, decide what you want from them. Write down your goals—maybe you want to improve your pronunciation, or to understand some aspect of grammar that puzzles you. Perhaps you want to ask questions that have arisen in the course of your own study, such as 'When do you use this word and not that word?' Save your questions for the class and bring them in your notebook.

Finding the right language class

The lessons you take can be cheap—they don't have to be first class. Even if they are second-rate, you can still benefit.

Classes are an excellent opportunity to improve your conversational skills, grammar and pronunciation. Friends may hesitate to tell you your grammar is wrong or your pronunciation is faulty. A teacher can tell you without risking offence.

Your instructor doesn't have to be a skilled or experienced teacher; if she or he is a native speaker of the language you are learning it will be enough for most purposes. A good option might be to find an overseas student to give you private lessons. Look in community-language newspapers for classified advertisements for private tuition. Many students are not only willing, but eager to teach their language to others to pay their way through college or university.

Group lessons

If there are other students you must be careful to be considerate, not demanding too much of the teacher's attention, but you can still ask questions. It may be worth your while to ask your teacher if you can pay for an extra half-hour to ask your questions.

Private lessons

Private lessons are a good alternative to a regular class, because you can determine the content of the lessons. If you are taking one-on-one private lessons, ask if you can provide your own textbook.

One-on-one pronunciation work

Private lessons are particularly good for working intensively on your pronunciation. As I related earlier, I once enrolled in a cheap Russian language course. I was the only student, so I felt free to ask my tutor for pronunciation drills. There are two Russian sounds for *l*—one hard and one soft—but I couldn't hear the difference between them. We spent one whole lesson on the words, *volny* (hard *l*) and *volny* (soft *l*). One meant 'free, available or vacant' and the other meant 'wave'. I practised saying them until I just about had it right. Sometimes my teacher would say, 'That's it. Say it again.' My next attempt would be wrong. It may have frustrated my teacher, but I was getting exactly what I needed.

★ ★ ★

Remember, most of your language study is done at home. Regular language classes are just another tool that you are using to master the language.

14

fourteen
δεκατέσσερα
quatorze
vierzehn
catorce
четырнадцать
empat belas
neljätoista

Meeting people

Spending a day with people who speak your target language and live its culture is in many ways similar to spending a day in their country. You can immerse yourself in the language and receive some very intensive training in speaking and understanding it. Meeting people is the most pleasant way to improve your language skills and it is also a good way to find out about a culture's social rules—what you should or shouldn't do.

On one particular occasion, my wife and I had a group of Germans in our home. I asked them in German, 'Would you like a cup of coffee?' One woman spoke up and said, '*Danke*' (thank you), so we gave her a cup. That was when we learnt that, in German, 'Thank you' means 'No, thank you'. If she had wanted a cup she would have said, 'Please', meaning, 'Yes, please'. This was a practical lesson, one which had not been included in our language textbooks.

Being with a group of people, all speaking your target language, forces you to converse in the language. It is the next best thing to a visit to the country (and a whole lot cheaper).

Meeting native speakers

There are many ways to get out and start meeting people. If a local newspaper is available in the language you are studying, buy a copy and look for contact details of cultural organisations which cater for people who speak this language. Telephone the appropriate embassy or consulate for suggestions if you can't find any information. You could visit a church, synagogue, mosque or temple, or a cultural centre or club. Look in the *Yellow Pages* for clubs or organisations that cater for your target language group.

Community-language papers and radio programs often announce special events that the public can attend. Most immigrant communities celebrate their home country's national day and various other festivals. Visit community-language or foreign-language bookshops for notices of events. Introduce yourself to people in the bookshop. Chat to them and begin a friendship. There is plenty going on out there if you look for it.

If you are learning a major language like German, French or Japanese, you also have the benefit of international organisations like the Goethe-Institut, Alliance Française and the Japan Foundation. Check them out and see what they offer. They usually have good libraries and a variety of language learning aids, as well as offering classes, special events, and the opportunity to meet people and speak the language. They are a great resource if you have questions about the language.

Attending functions

Visiting functions at which people will be speaking in your target language and trying out your skills is certainly an adventure.

It is possible to prepare for this adventure. A useful method is to hold a conversation with yourself in the language to force yourself to think in the language. I sometimes used to drive to France from Germany. I was used to speaking and thinking in German, so to 'switch' my mind to French I would speak to myself in French as I approached the border. Do the same when you are visiting a club, church, cultural centre or restaurant. That way, you won't be tongue-tied if someone speaks to you unexpectedly.

When you are first introduced to people, try to learn their names immediately. Write the new names down if necessary, or have someone write them down for you. Try to use these names as you make conversation, and be sure you get them right—ask if you are saying them correctly.

To break the ice, you might like to ask about practices you find interesting: 'Can you explain to me why everybody seems to be …?' Usually, people are pleased to answer these kinds of questions. Take the opportunity to offer others drinks or refreshments in their own language. Try to fit in and speak the language as much as you can. People will appreciate your effort—learning someone's language is an act of friendship.

When you attend functions, by all means be ready to ask questions, but don't take up too much of anyone's time with them. People are there to enjoy themselves. If you do have a chance to ask your language questions, try to dispense with them quickly, and be profuse in your thanks.

Making friends

Newcomers to your country may be just as keen to make friends with locals and English-speakers as you are to meet native speakers of your target language. If you make a friend at a function, you can offer to help them negotiate the intricacies of living in your country. You can follow up with personal visits and often help each other with your language studies.

Making new friends adds to the fun of the adventure.

Visit the country

A visit to a country in which your target language is spoken is great if you can manage it. There is nothing like buying a ticket on a bus or ordering a meal to give you practice and confidence in using a language, and travelling is the best way to meet native speakers.

Different language groups obviously have different cultures, and even within a language group you will find differences. Many languages, such as Spanish, French and English, are spoken by people of very different cultures. It is a good idea to learn as much as possible about the country you will be visiting, its people and their culture *before* you go. I see it as an essential part of learning the language.

Get as much travel information as possible from the internet before you go. Download maps and articles on customs and culture. Visit tourism sites and try to find personal advice from travellers who have been to the country you plan to visit. Government tourism pages are usually helpful here. Get facts and figures about the country. Which languages are spoken and by whom? Which religions are practised and by how many people? What is the population of the country, of the main cities? What is the main means of transport? How should you dress? Should you cover your head or leave it uncovered? Should you remove your shoes before entering someone's house?

Not all of this information is included in a language course. You are more likely to find it on the internet and in travel guides.

If you are travelling to a country for business reasons, it is essential you learn as much as possible about the culture and traditions of the country. This seems self-evident, but I have seen many people visit a country and make the most elementary mistakes, ruining any chance of success. It is a good idea to ask local people you will be working with for advice in this area. Tell them you don't understand the culture of the country very well and ask for their help and advice. Ask them to excuse in advance any mistakes you might make. Also, when you leave the country, apologise for any mistakes you might have made. I have found this to be a good practice. You can avoid unpleasant situations in the country if you are prepared and greatly increase your chances of forming both good working relationships and friendships with the people you meet.

Get out into your local community

Visiting the country is ideal, of course, but in the meantime, the next best thing is a visit to your local communities which use your target language. Most Australian capital cities have a Chinatown; many have areas special to the Greek, Italian and Vietnamese communities and to many other national groups. There are religious gathering places and clubs catering for speakers of various languages. Frequent these places in your own city, and find someone to talk to. Are you learning Vietnamese? Visit a Vietnamese restaurant or a store run by Vietnamese people where you can practise your skills. If you are learning German, French, Thai, Greek, Italian, Chinese or Vietnamese, there are plenty of restaurants you can visit to practise speaking the language.

This is a fun way to immerse yourself in the language. Make use of the opportunities. There are plenty if you look for them.

Don't worry about making mistakes

People are usually not just willing but very keen to talk with others who are making the effort to learn their language. They will often help you to improve your language skills. Don't worry about making mistakes and don't be embarrassed. Learning a language is not a competition and no-one is going to punish you if you get your verb wrong or if you have difficulty making yourself understood.

When I was driving with my family through Poland, it was a hot day so I stopped to buy some ice-cream. The storekeeper didn't understand what I was saying. I made lapping motions with my tongue and then drew a picture of an ice-cream cone. His face lit up with understanding and he said the word the way I should have. Polish has two letters and sounds for *l* and I had used the wrong one. Everyone else in the shop was listening and wanted to know what I was after. Often, in this kind of situation, people will try to be helpful, and will say, 'I think he wants …' Don't be frightened by these kinds of situations—treat them as fun.

I was sitting in an open air Chinese restaurant in Singapore and I wanted an iced chocolate drink. The people at my table explained I should ask for a Milo *peng* or Milo *ping*. (The second word seemed to be pronounced midway between these two options.) When the waiter came I ordered my drink in Chinese, much to the amusement and pleasure of the other people at the table.

On a later occasion, I was at an outdoor Chinese restaurant by myself and tried this again. I asked for Milo *peng*. The waiter had no idea what I was saying. I repeated my request and he still didn't understand. I then told him in English and asked him how I should have said it. He was happy to help. The way he pronounced the word sounded almost the same to me as the way I had said it, but I took note as well as I could of the subtle difference.

My knowledge of Chinese has never progressed beyond the absolute basic polite expressions, but saying 'hello', 'please', 'thank you' and 'goodbye' in Chinese has made me many friends. (And I can order a drink of iced Milo in Chinese!)

Grammar

15

fifteen
δεκαπέντε
quinze
fünfzehn
quince
пятнадцать
lima belas
viisitoista

Many people take fright at the mention of the word 'grammar', but there is no need to. Every time we speak we are using grammar, whether we know it or not. Some knowledge of grammar is essential if you want to speak any language, including your own. You may not understand why you say some things the way you do, but you are certainly using grammar to some degree.

You automatically say 'I am', 'you are', and 'he is' or 'she is'. You change the form of the verb without thinking of any rules: you say 'I am' rather than 'I are' or 'I is' just because it *sounds* right. If you had to think of the correct rules before producing every sentence you utter, you would never say anything, and yet this is the approach many classes and textbooks take. They want to start you on grammar before you say anything.

It *is* necessary to understand grammar to understand and use any language properly, but we will learn it using the method we have discussed in earlier chapters. We will use the language first—we will read it, hear it and speak it—then we will learn the rules. This is how we learnt our own language. (Note though, that the way you learnt your own language is not necessarily the best method—it should in fact be possible to learn a new language well in just months, not years.)

Don't worry about learning rules or declensions by heart. The first step is to understand and to recognise the rules. Much will come simply with use.

Memorise useful sentences that use the rule you want to learn. When I was first in Germany I spoke terrible German, but I would sometimes suddenly insert sentences that were elegantly constructed into my general flow of speech. It must have puzzled my listeners. These sentences were straight from my Assimil German course. In using them, I was also using the rule concerning the position of the verb in the sentence, long before I had learnt it formally. That made it much easier to learn this rule when I eventually did so. First I did it—then I learnt *why* I was doing it. Learning grammar first can actually slow down the process of speaking a language. Speak the language first and then learn the rules.

If you have to think of the correct sentence construction and correct grammar before you open your mouth to say something in your target language then you haven't really learnt the language. You can never be comfortable translating your thoughts from English (or any other mother tongue) into your target language. You need to think directly in the language. Where correct grammar and sentence construction are concerned, you just need to let things flow. That is why, when I travel to a country where they speak a language other than the one I have been using, I spend half an hour or so thinking in the new language and speaking to myself. I am tuning my mind to the language I will be using.

As I noted in chapter 9, the current belief is that our brains have a different language centre for each language that we know. It is only when you start to think in a language and stop translating what you are saying from your own language that the new language centre is developed. Children do this naturally. Adults generally have to work at it. For this reason, I advocate passive learning of the language first, before the formal learning of grammar. You should just recognise the rules at first. By all means, read the rules of grammar as you learn the language, but only for the purpose of recognising them as you see them applied. You are under no obligation to remember everything, just understand at first and recognise.

Grammar can be fun. I actually enjoyed learning English grammar at school. I liked things to make sense. I still like to ask questions and to know why we do things.

Some people travel to a foreign country and say they hate it—everything is so different. If everything were the same, though, you might as well stay home. It is the differences that make travel interesting. I love the differences. When I travel to a new country I ask questions all the time. I want to know what everything is, why they do things the way they do. The differences intrigue me. The same goes for the grammar of a foreign language. The differences can be fun to learn.

For example, many English-speakers are taught not to use a double negative, because a double negative makes a positive. This is true. Take the sentence, 'I have no money.' The meaning is clear. The opposite of this sentence would be, 'I don't have no money,' meaning, 'It is not true that I have no money'—in other words, 'I do have money'. However, in Afrikaans, people use double negatives to convey a negative meaning all the time—it is a standard part of the language.

A linguistics professor was addressing his students and said, 'A double negative in English will actually give you a positive, but a double positive can't give a negative.'

A cynical voice was heard from the back of the room, 'Yeah, sure.'

Each language applies its rules differently. Here is another example. In English, strict grammarians tell us that we should say, 'It is I.' In German you would say, *Es bin ich*—literally, 'It is I'—as well. In French, on the other hand, you say, *C'est moi*, or 'It [this] is me'. Most people speaking English would probably say, 'It's me,' and no-one would take any notice, but get it wrong in German or French and you sound like you are horribly mangling the language. Passive learning would take care of this for you, saving you from the necessity of formally learning the rule.

We will attack the grammar of the language we are learning using a method similar to that taught in the Assimil language programs, discussed in chapter 8. With the Assimil language courses, you work through the first two months quickly, learning basic words and sentence construction, much the way you learnt your own language. You tune your ear and your mind to the sound and rhythm of the language. You learn to think in the language. Then they begin what they call the 'second wave'. You go back to lesson one and do the grammar exercises. Because you are now familiar with the words and sentence construction, the exercises are now easy. It is the same with your own language—'I are hungry' just doesn't sound right. So, you continue to work with the grammar two months behind where you are with the language.

We will do the same with our textbooks. Before, we read the grammar and tried a few exercises to check that we understood what they were teaching. We almost ignored the grammar sections and exercises.

Now we do the exercises from about ten lessons back, so as we work on lesson 11 we are doing the grammar exercises for lesson 1. You can make the grammar exercises twenty lessons behind if you like. It will depend on the textbook you are using. As we forge ahead with lesson 16 we are doing the grammar for lesson 6. That should make the grammar easy and take away most of the drudgery.

The importance of grammar

I think correct use of language (especially your own) is essential. My family accuses me of being pedantic. It is probably true. If we are sloppy in the way we use language, our arguments and logic are inclined to be sloppy. We may delude ourselves in our thinking. Also, you make a bad impression when you use poor grammar. People don't just think you are uneducated, they think you are unintelligent as well. It is worth the effort to learn the correct grammar when you are learning a foreign language.

A bonus is that as you learn the grammar for your new language, your understanding of English grammar will improve as well.

I have a good friend, a schoolteacher, who married a Russian and started taking Russian lessons. She said to me, 'I didn't know I was so ignorant of English grammar. You need to know your own grammar to learn Russian.' So it is for any language. You must have some knowledge of grammar.

A simple grammar lesson

The following short summary of grammar covers the basics that you will need to know to master your next language fully. You don't need to learn or memorise this information; you can refer to it as you need it.

Sentences and phrases

A *sentence* is a group of words that makes complete sense.

A *phrase* is two or more words in sequence, forming a unit within a sentence.

Subjects and predicates

Every sentence has a *subject* and a *predicate*.

The subject is the part of the sentence that tells you what or who is doing or being.

The predicate tells you what is happening, to whom, and other details about the action or being.

'He went' is a simple sentence. 'He' is the subject and 'went' is the predicate.

The sentence, 'He went to school,' has the same subject ('he'), but it has a longer predicate ('went to school'), this time giving you a bit more information about what he did.

The sentence, 'Did he go?' has 'he' as the subject and 'did go' as the predicate.

Objects

Some sentences have *objects* as well as a subject. In the sentence, 'She rode the bike, 'she' is the subject and 'bike' is the object. The object is the thing or person affected by the action of the subject.

Objects can be *direct* or *indirect*. In the sentence, 'She rode the bike to the park,' 'bike' is the direct object. 'Park' is the indirect object.

Nouns

A *noun* is a 'name' word. A noun can be something tangible, like 'table', 'book', or 'oven', or something intangible, like 'love', 'justice' and 'virtue'. A *proper noun* is the name of a particular person or animal, or the name of a particular thing, such as a country or a language. 'Jack', 'Wendy', 'Fido', 'Australia' and 'English' are all proper nouns.

Singular and plural nouns

In English the *plural* form of a *singular* noun is formed by adding an *s*, though there are exceptions. If a word ends in an *s* sound, you add *es*. This rule also applies to words ending in *sh* and *ch*. There are some words which have irregular plural forms, like 'child' (children) and 'knife' (knives). Each language has its rules and its exceptions to the rule. In Indonesian you say a word twice to show that it is plural. In writing, you might just write a *2* after the singular form of the noun. For example, *orang* means 'person' and *orang2* means 'people'. Nouns in some languages have no plural form at all, and it is context alone which specifies whether they are singular or plural.

Gender

As I observed in chapter 9, in most languages, nouns are either masculine or feminine. It doesn't matter if the word in question represents an object such as a book or ball; it will be either masculine or feminine. In some languages there is a third gender, neuter. A word's ending will generally tell its gender. For instance, the German words for 'girl' (*Mädchen*), and 'Miss' (*Fräulein*), are not feminine, as you might expect, but neuter, because all words ending in *-chen* and *-lein* are neuter. When you learn the rules, it all becomes a little easier. Getting the gender right is important, but if you make a mistake you will still be understood.

I remember telling a fellow English teacher in Germany that I still made mistakes with declensions and genders. She told me she had never noticed. I said, 'That's because when I am in doubt, I mumble.' She thought it was a great joke and the story soon went around the entire teaching staff, but it was true.

I also suspect that she was simply being polite, telling me she hadn't picked up my mistakes. But, even with my mistakes, my command of German was not only good enough to teach in a German school but to speak in public. Some of my mistakes probably added humour to my presentations. You will inevitably make mistakes, but don't worry too much about them, even as you strive for perfection.

Pronouns

A *pronoun* is a word that is used instead of a noun. 'I', 'you', 'it', 'he', and 'she' are all examples of pronouns.

Most language books and courses teach the first, second and third person pronouns very early on.

The first, second and third person singular pronouns in English are as follows:

- I/me (first person)

- you (second person)

- he/him, she/her, it (third person)

The plural pronouns are:

- we/us (first person)

- you (second person)

- they/them (third person)

Adjectives

An *adjective* is a word which describes a noun. 'Short', 'fat', 'red', 'smooth' and 'happy' are examples of adjectives.

Verbs

A *verb* is usually a word that describes some kind of action. Words like 'do', 'see', 'hear', 'say', 'hit', 'write', 'run' and 'walk' are verbs.

Even the words 'be' and 'have' are verbs; in fact, they are the two most important words in most languages. (Interestingly, Russian uses neither in the present tense, with one exception: to say, 'I have a pencil' in Russian, you would say, 'At me is pencil.')

The *infinitive* is the basic form of the verb, sometimes known as the *dictionary form*, because it is the form you will find in the dictionary. In English, a verb in its infinitive form is preceded by the word 'to', as in the verbs, 'to go', 'to see' and 'to have'.

Tense

Tense is used to indicate when the action described by a verb took place. It can also refer to the state of the action. English uses two *auxiliary* or 'helper' verbs to form some tenses — 'to be' and 'to have'. Verbs change according to tense. An illustration is given in table 15.1, overleaf, which uses the verb 'to fly' as an example.

Voice

A verb can be in the *active* or the *passive* voice. In an active construction, the subject carries out the action described by the verb. In the sentence, 'I flew the plane', the verb is in the active voice. 'I' is the subject — the person flying the plane.

In a passive construction, the subject has the action described by the verb *done to it*. In the sentence, 'The plane was flown by me', the verb is in the passive voice.

Adverbs

An *adverb* is a word that describes a verb. In English, adverbs mainly end in -*ly*. For example, in the sentence, 'He drank the water slowly', the word 'slowly' tells you about the drinking; it doesn't describe the drinker or the water. 'Quickly', 'smoothly' and 'happily' are all examples of adverbs.

Table 15.1: different forms of the verb 'to fly'

Verb: to fly	Tense
I fly.	simple present
I am flying.	continuous present
I flew.	simple past
I was flying. I used to fly.	continuous past
I have flown.	perfect
I had flown.	complete past
I have been flying.	perfect continuous
I had been flying.	continuous complete past
I shall fly, I will fly.	simple future
I shall be flying. I will be flying.	continuous future
I shall have flown.	future perfect
I shall have been flying. I will have been flying.	future perfect continuous

Prepositions

In English, a *preposition* is a word placed in front of a noun that tells you about the noun's relationship to other words in the sentence. Words like 'with', 'to', 'by', 'before', 'after', 'in' and 'over' are all prepositions. 'Near the bank', 'to the school' and 'with his mother' are all examples of the use of prepositions. (You may remember the preposition diagram from chapter 4—if not, refer back to page 31.)

Conjunctions

A *conjunction* joins sentences, phrases and words together. The word 'and' is the most common conjunction. 'But' and 'because' are two further examples.

Articles

The English words 'the', 'a' and 'an' are all *articles*. 'The' is known as the *definite article* and 'a' and 'an' are *indefinite articles*. They are words used to determine or describe the 'scope' of a noun. If you say 'a book', you might mean any book, but when you say 'the book', the listener knows it is not just any book you are talking about; it is *the* book, a particular book, the book we have been discussing.

Some languages don't have an indefinite article, and some languages don't have either definite or indefinite articles.

Cases

The function or role of a noun or a pronoun in a sentence is known as its *case*. A noun which is the subject of a sentence is in the *nominative* case. For example, in a sentence such as 'You are right' or 'You have a new hat', the word 'you' is the subject, so it is in the nominative case.

A noun which is the direct object of a sentence is in the *accusative* case. In the sentences 'I see you' or 'I hit you', the word 'you' is the direct object, so it is in the accusative case.

Native speakers can get by in English without understanding cases at all. However, an understanding of case is vital to the study of some languages.

In many languages, the form of a noun or a pronoun might change according to its case. In others, the article (the word for 'the' or 'a' which precedes the noun) might change. The study of some languages, such as German and Latin, will require that you learn the *dative* case, which applies to the indirect object of a verb. The *genitive* case indicates the owner of the noun in question. These simply have to be learnt for some languages—there is no way out of it.

I remember thinking it was unfair that German and English had different rules about case. I didn't like the complex German rules, but I had to live with them or speak bad German. German children learn the correct grammar with use—and I have too. You shouldn't be intimidated or frightened by unfamiliar grammatical concepts. When you reach the second wave, or active part of your study, much of the grammar will have sorted itself out in your mind and it will come naturally to you.

Word order

In English, word order is important. The two sentences, 'The man bit the dog' and 'The dog bit the man' obviously have different meanings. However, in some languages, it is not the *order* of the words that tells you who did the biting and who was bitten, but the *endings* on the words. In some languages, the word for 'dog' would change to let you know it was the dog that was bitten or doing the biting; in other languages, it would be the word for 'the' that would change. In some languages, a marker word would be inserted to let the listener know who did what to whom. To learn this, you have to learn and understand cases (which we discussed earlier).

In many languages, including Spanish and Italian, the adjective follows the noun it modifies. You would say 'the car red' instead of 'the red car', or 'the house big', instead of 'the big house'.

In others, the position of the verb in the sentence is different to that which English-speakers are used to. I have heard people complain that you have to wait forever until you hear the main verb in a German sentence. In English we say, 'I believe I would rather watch television.' In German this would be, 'I believe that I rather television watch would.'

Learning new rules may seem daunting but, once you have begun, many of these unfamiliar patterns or structures will start to seem natural, and you will soon start to use them automatically. As you progress with the language, you will find you are constructing your sentences correctly without thinking about it.

Putting grammar into practice

Let's revise our discussion of grammar by looking at the sentence, 'The little girl hit the ball hard.'

- 'The young girl' is the subject.

- 'Hit the ball hard' is the predicate.

- 'The' is the definite article.

- 'Young' is an adjective describing the girl.

- 'Girl' is a noun. It is in the nominative case, because it is the subject of the sentence.

- 'Hit' is the verb. It is in the past simple tense and the active voice.

- 'Ball' is another noun. It is the accusative case, because it is the object of the sentence. It is the thing that is hit.

- 'Hard' is an adverb. It doesn't describe the nouns in the sentence (the girl or the ball); it describes the verb, 'hit'. It tells you how the ball was hit.

Take as another, slightly more complex example the sentence, 'The girl hit the ball over the fence':

- The 'girl' is the subject.

- 'Hit the ball over the fence' is the predicate.

- The ball is the direct object. It tells you *what* the girl hit.

- Over the fence is the *indirect object*. It is the *dative case*. It tells you what happened to the direct object, in this case, *where* she hit it.

If you had trouble following any of the above explanations, don't worry too much. Your textbooks will explain as you learn. What you don't understand in one text may be quite clear in another. I suggest you invest in a simple English grammar book and another grammar book for the language you are learning. With our multipronged attack, understanding of grammar is not essential at the beginning, but you need to understand it eventually. Grammar is essential if you want to learn a foreign language well.

To summarise, the way to master the grammar of the language you are learning is to read the explanations in your textbook as you go during the passive learning stage, simply noting them, without worrying about memorising rules of grammar. Then, when you arrive at the active stage (a dozen or so lessons behind your passive learning study), you do some of the grammar exercises. Even then, I wouldn't bother too much about memorising word endings and verb forms—I count on my use of the correct sentences from my textbooks to impress the rules in my mind unconsciously, just as I did when I learnt English as a child.

Plan your own immersion program 16

sixteen
δεκαέξι
seize
sechzehn
dieciséis
шестнадцать
enam belas
kuusitoista

When you have made some progress in your studies and have material to review, plan a day of total immersion in the language. By spending a whole day speaking the language and thinking in the language, you will make huge progress. It is the next best thing to being in a country in which your target language is spoken. It can in fact be better than 'being there', if you spend the time actually learning, because you don't necessarily spend your time learning the language when you live in a foreign country. Many people live in a country for years without ever learning the language.

The benefits of immersion days

When I first arrived in Germany, I discovered I could understand the spoken language quite well, but I couldn't understand radio news broadcasts. They used a different, more formal, language. After a while, though, I found I could follow the news broadcasts quite well. Understanding comes eventually. I also found at first that conversing in German would tire me. After speaking with friends for a while my concentration would begin to flag. My friends thought it hilarious that, late at night, my command of the language would worsen and I would have trouble expressing myself. Also, I found that listening to a lecture given in German used to tire me easily, because I had to concentrate at a higher level than normal. Everyone was amused one time when I asked a lecturer to say anything important in the first ten minutes of his talk. After that I couldn't guarantee I would be listening or, at least, concentrating.

My experience has been similar with other languages. I found I would tire after having to concentrate on speaking French, Russian or Dutch for an hour or so. The only advice I can give is to immerse yourself in the language as much as you can *before* you need to use it in real life. As you think in the language and practise using the language you will become more proficient and will soon find that your level of concentration is not so critical. Once you are a little more comfortable thinking in the language, you don't have to concentrate so much on sentence construction.

All of this is part of the process of learning a language. Don't be troubled by it—just plan for it. By having immersion days, you can minimise problems, dealing with them as much as possible while you are still learning at home.

Preparing for an immersion day

You need to plan your immersion day in advance and have your tools ready. Have a good selection of recorded music and audio books in addition to your teaching material. (If you ever feel you are being swamped in the language and need a break, you can play this music as you take a coffee break or a meal break.) Check whether there are any programs on community-language radio that you can listen to on the day, even if they will only be background noise to set the mood. If there is a film in the language or a radio broadcast scheduled for the day, make watching these a part of your schedule, or organise some videos or DVDs for the occasion.

You need to have interesting reading matter ready, as well as your textbooks and phrasebooks. Have magazines, joke books and comic books on hand, or maybe an interesting novel. It is a good idea to have something special you have saved up for yourself for the day. It can be a new book, a comic book, a video in the language—anything that you think you will enjoy.

Buy some food that you can treat yourself with at mealtimes. When I was learning French I bought baguettes to eat with a big cup of coffee (French-style). Treat yourself to the cuisine of the culture of your language. You can fool yourself into thinking you are actually in the country.

Suggested plan

Here are some suggestions about how to plan your day.

Over breakfast, play music from the country in the background while you eat. You can also play your language tape, reviewing old lessons in the background while you finish your meal.

Next, go to work with your textbooks. Begin a new page or section in your language notebook to write everything you learn on the day. That way you can look back when it is over and point to specific gains you have made. Do a lesson from each textbook. Do some written exercises.

You will spend much of your time reviewing past lessons in your textbooks and trying some of the early exercises, but be sure to try some new lessons so that you can say you have learnt something new. Also, read through your grammar book just for fun. It will give you new insight into how the language works.

After an hour or so, break for coffee. As you make your coffee, speak to yourself in the language. 'Let's make some coffee. Would you like a cup of coffee? Do you take milk and sugar? What would you like with the coffee? Would you like some cake? What will we read?' While you drink your coffee, read a joke book or a comic book: 'Let's read Tintin.'

Holding a conversation with yourself gives you practice speaking the language. Speak out loud. There is no-one around to think you are strange.

You might choose to spend some time on the internet, but be careful to stick to your plan. Write an email in your target language, or visit some websites. If you don't have anyone else to write to, send the contact person at one of these websites an email.

If you are interested in a sport or even a board game or card game, learn the vocabulary you would need to participate in it or play it with others using your target language. This can be a fun activity. I can play chess games notated in almost any language. It is not difficult, even though it may sound impressive.

At lunchtime, follow the same routine as your morning coffee break. Keep up a running conversation with yourself and play music or language tapes in the background.

You should begin your afternoon with your textbooks again, and keep going as long as you can take it. Then vary your reading and listening as much as you can. I would spend some time again reading a grammar book.

When you are feeling tired, give yourself your treat. Watch the video or read the book you have set aside for the day.

Afterwards, review what you have learned during the day. Your notebook will help you here. Go over your new grammar, vocabulary, and any other gains you feel you have made.

For your evening meal you might like to visit a restaurant where you can eat food typical of the country or culture you are interested in and speak to the waiters in your target language.

If you have your meal at home, play an internet radio station broadcasting in your target language in the background as you eat. You are practising to live in the country.

After your meal, you can watch a movie in the language or do some light reading—maybe a comic.

By the end of the day you should be a long way further forward in your language study. You should be thinking in the language and you should be ready to go to bed and dream in the language. You will find that you will begin to dream in the language or dream you are speaking with someone in the language.

Immersion-day outings

The day of total immersion I have just outlined was all planned to take place inside your home. As an alternative, you may wish to make a visit to a cultural function into a day or evening of total immersion. Check out community-language schools, clubs and religious and political organisations; ask for a copy of their newsletter and check out any social functions. Gatherings at which everyone meets to enjoy themselves and celebrate are obviously the best choice. In this case, however, you will not be in charge of the learning opportunities and you may not accomplish as much as you would during a day at home. Try both kinds of immersion programs. Plan some days at home and some at other suitable venues. Take advantage of everything that will help.

Mini–immersion days

Sometimes it may not be feasible to have an immersion day in the near future, but you can always have a mini–immersion day if you have a morning, afternoon or evening free. If you can spend four, six or even eight hours immersed in the language at a time, you can make great progress. You will be surprised at how much you can accomplish. I think that having your brain switch to thinking in the language and processing the language directly is the biggest gain.

17

seventeen
δεκαεπτά
dix-sept
siebzehn
diecisiete
семнадцать
tujuh belas
seitsemäntoista

What if you just don't feel like it?

There will be days when you feel you just can't make the effort to study your new language. Accept this, and have a contingency plan for these days. I would make a commitment, however, that there will be never more than two of these days in a week and never two days running.

Your contingency plan

What should you do on those days when you are feeling too lazy to exercise your mind?

The day is not lost. Simply play your language study cassette or CD in the background as you go about other business, so you are revising your previous work. You could go back over a lesson in your textbook—revising an old lesson is not hard work.

Then take a break and indulge yourself. Play some of your favourite recordings in the language. Eat at your favourite restaurant serving food from the country or culture you are learning about. Read a comic book or joke book in the language. As you do so, you motivate yourself to work at your target language again.

It is actually a good policy to reward your efforts. When you have worked particularly hard and achieved a lot, give yourself a treat. In other words, bribe yourself to do the right thing. Make plans for your study time: *I will accomplish this today and then reward myself with* …

In fact, you can put aside some treats and bribes for your 'don't feel like it' days. Have a hoard of comic books, joke books, music, and videos stashed away for some 'easy' practice on the days you don't feel like making a proper effort and sticking to your study routine.

Discouragement

What do you do when you feel discouraged? Discouragement will set in at different times in the learning of any language — it is simply a normal part of the process.

Sometimes you will be discouraged because you don't seem to be making much progress. Sometimes it is the result of tackling a task that is beyond you at present.

As a beginner learning Russian, I felt despair several times when I was confronted with new grammar which seemed specifically designed to make the job of mastering the language impossible. Sometimes I wished I had never begun my study of Russian. The first time I felt like giving up, the obstacles just seemed insurmountable, but I decided to continue anyway and hoped the problem would sort itself out as I kept up my pace and tackled new lessons. This is good general advice. Just keep going. Make a note of your difficulty and steam ahead anyway. There is no law that says you can't go on to the next lesson until you have mastered the current one. Persevere with the new stuff; then, when you are feeling more cheerful, get hold of some grammar books or do an internet search and look for answers to your earlier problem.

Try not to be discouraged by others' remarks, and don't compare your progress with anybody else's. Language learning is not a contest. You are not competing with anyone else. You have set yourself goals and you are working towards achieving them. If it seems that your original goals were unrealistic, modify them. They don't have to be written in concrete.

I still haven't resolved all of my questions on Russian grammar and I don't know if I can tell the difference yet between hard-*l volny* and soft-*l volny*. I carry on regardless: I find I can still get by in the language and I treat myself to immersion days from time to time. I don't worry too much about minor hurdles.

This is one of the benefits of using the first and second wave approach. You don't have to understand all of the grammar during the first wave. The theory is that the difficulties will sort themselves out by the time you reach the second wave or active stage of your study.

Often, discouragement sets in because we are looking for perfection in our knowledge of the language. Very few people are perfect in their own language, so don't let your weaknesses get you down.

I have never managed to learn to pronounce the German *e* properly. I have discovered that I pronounce the German *e* the same way it is pronounced in the Swabian dialect. The Swabians manage all right without the 'pure' or High German pronunciation, and so do I. I just have a slight Swabian accent—no-one minds.

Accept the fact that you feel frustrated and discouraged, and continue on with your studies anyway. Make a pact with yourself that you will do something every day in your target language, even if it is only just revising your language recordings or revising old lessons in your textbook—at least you will not be going backwards. Some of my early problems learning Russian now seem trivial and I wonder why I ever had any difficulty. It will be the same for you.

eighteen
δεκαοκτώ
dix-huit
achtzehn
dieciocho
восемнадцать
delapan belas
kahdeksantoista

Using the internet

18

The internet has changed our lives forever. A huge store of information is now accessible to anyone, no matter where they live, so long as they have access to the internet. The internet opens up a wealth of opportunities to anyone who seriously wants to learn another language.

In this chapter, I look at the language-learning materials and resources available online. Some of the websites I mention may no longer exist by the time you read this book—websites come and go. If you find the web address I have quoted results in an error message, please don't give up. There will be other pages you can find that will serve a similar purpose. I believe, though, that the web addresses I have provided are likely to be around for a while.

Getting started: using search engines

You can find enormous amounts of useful information and material on the internet just by doing an ordinary English-language search. However, you can also use Google, AltaVista, Yahoo or WebCrawler, (or perhaps your own favourite search engine) to look for pages in the language of your choice. This is very easy to do;

for example, on the Google home page, you click on 'preferences' and stipulate that you want to search only for pages in Arabic or Afrikaans, then save this preference. I have often done this to limit searches to pages in my target language.

Searching foreign-language pages will usually work even if your search words are in English, but you can, of course, use a dictionary to find strategic terms in your target language. Don't forget to reset the preferences on Google when you have finished your search.

Language courses on the internet

Let us say you want to learn Portuguese. You can simply type, 'learn Portuguese' into a search engine and it will find thousands of appropriate websites for you. These websites will offer all kinds of texts to print out and read, grammar reference resources, audio materials and short teaching videos you can download and play back to your heart's content.

You can often find complete language courses on the internet with lessons, grammar and audio files that you can download for free. There will undoubtedly be something available for the language you want to learn. I have downloaded entire courses in Malay and Spanish and language-learning materials for many other languages.

Recommended sites and courses

There is no end to the excellent resources available on the web. The following recommendations should by no means be considered exhaustive. These are just a few sites and courses I have found useful myself. There are serious language programs being offered. All you have to do is look for them.

Word2Word

Probably the most comprehensive site listing free online language courses is <www.word2word.com/coursead.html>. I recommend making this the first site you visit, as it lists web resources for many languages. It is worth checking out to find study materials for your target language. It also lists sites from which you can download free software for typing or word processing in your target language.

Languages-on-the-web

Another excellent site I highly recommend is <www.languages-on-the-web.com>. It has resources in many languages, from Afrikaans, Ancient Greek and Egyptian, to Greenlandic, Yiddish and Zulu, as well as more widely spoken languages. The people who put this site together have taken a number of short stories and published them in different languages. Each translation is presented alongside the original English text of the story, so you can see both versions at once. The stories make easy and pleasant reading. You can print them to take with you to learn while you commute or simply to use as fun learning exercises. The site has links to other useful online resources for each individual language represented, sorted into categories including:

- general links

- interesting sites

- software, books and tapes

- translators and interpreters

- schools, courses and institutions.

Links are also provided to online resources including:

- bilingual texts

- courses

- grammar references

- dictionaries

- newspapers and magazines

- radio and TV stations

- sites focused on culture, religion, literature, arts and music.

Synergy Spanish

If you are learning Spanish, then the Synergy Spanish language program is an excellent choice. The program is first-class and inexpensive, but it is best to have a fast internet connection to download the audio. I have a slower modem connection, but I was able to download the audio part of the program an hour or so at a time over several days. You can download the first four lessons in the textbook for free to try it out. You will be amazed at what you can say in Spanish after only four lessons: the program teaches you how to get the most mileage from the least number of words. Visit <www.synergyspanish.com> to find out more.

Learn Greek Online

At <www.kypros.org/Greek>, it is possible to download a complete Greek course with more than 100 lessons and real audio files. This is an excellent, high-quality course—and it is free.

UK India

At <www.ukindia.com>, you will find downloadable material for a number of Indian and Middle Eastern languages. As I noted in chapter 6, it is worth a visit if you are learning languages such as

Hindi, Arabic, Hebrew or Sanskrit. Don't just visit the website, check out its links to other sites as well.

Online dictionaries

Online and electronic dictionaries are a great resource. It is easier to search for the meaning of a word when you are at your computer or on the internet if you can just click on the dictionary icon and type in the word than it is to consult your dictionary and find the correct page. I have found them very useful. At <www.freelang.net> you will find dictionaries for seventy-nine languages you can download to your computer completely free.

Online reading materials

In chapter 12, I discussed various kinds of reading materials, but I believe it is worth making special mention of online materials.

Online news services

Online newspapers are a fantastic resource. In addition to news articles, they have cartoons, short humorous pieces and other items of interest. It can be a good idea to make the newspaper of your choice your home page. That way, when you log on to the internet you automatically see the news headlines in your target language. If you don't know where to start, just search for 'international newspaper directory'. There are many good directories, and these should help you find a suitable publication.

The BBC and Voice of America websites and many other international media organisations have news pages and headlines in multiple languages.

General reading

Other good resources are information pages on the country or countries in which your target language is spoken, their people and their cultures. These pages are usually travel related, but often give valuable information on the language as well.

If you are looking for a website that covers a particular subject in your target language, do searches by typing in a key word in the language you are learning. If the word is common to several languages, you can narrow the search to your language by changing the Google language preferences. This is a good way to improve your knowledge of the language on technical or specialist topics.

Also, the 'Languages on the Web' website mentioned earlier in this chapter has easy reading material in many languages. I highly recommend you visit this website to check out its resources for your language.

E-books and e-zines

E-books and e-zines (electronic books and magazines) are another option. Many are available for free; others are for subscribers only.

Books

If you hunt around on the internet, you are sure to find e-books in your target language to download. A good place to start might be the foreign languages section of the Online Books Page hosted by the University of Pennsylvania Library at <http://onlinebooks. library.upenn.edu/archives.html#foreign>.

Magazines

Search for e-zines that cater for your interests. There are online publications on virtually any subject: look for the webpages of magazines that cover your favourite hobby or sport. This will help you expand your vocabulary in your area of interest. You can read them at your desk or on your laptop, or print out the pages that interest you and take them with you when you travel or to read in your coffee breaks.

Web translations

Some search engines and other websites offer web-based automatic translation tools. AltaVista's translation tool is called Babel Fish and you can find it at <http://babelfish.altavista.com>. Babel Fish allows you to type in text to be translated directly and can also translate whole webpages if you insert the web address. Google offers similar tools.

These translation options are on the internet and are available to anyone for free—so use them! They are great for translating documents relevant to your work or study needs into the language. Please note, though, that the translations such services provide should only be used as a guide or as an aid to understanding—they aren't always accurate. I certainly wouldn't just write a letter or report in English and let Google or AltaVista do the translation. However, despite the mistakes in the translations these free online services provide, they give you a start—something to work from. This is not a substitute for writing something yourself, but it will help you to write better letters and reports.

A good way to test the validity of the translation is to have the website translate your document back into English once you have finished it. You will find some strange, and sometimes hilarious, changes to your writing.

If you install SlimBrowser on your computer as well as your usual browser software, you will be able to translate foreign webpages at the click of your mouse. The menu at the top of the screen offers the option of translating a page into English. Click on the button and you will see the page translated into English in seconds. SlimBrowser can be downloaded free at <http://flashpeak.com>. The file is quite small, only one and a half megabytes, and installs easily, quickly and automatically.

Again, you will often find that individual words have been translated rather than the sense of the article, and the result can be quite difficult to read. For example, when I used SlimBrowser to translate an article about Fidel Castro, it called him 'Fidel I castrate'. Apparently, *castro* means, 'I castrate' in Spanish. I hadn't come across *that* in my Spanish lessons, so I learnt something new, but I am not sure where or when I will have the chance to use this knowledge.

Internet radio

It wasn't so long ago that the only option was to listen on short wave; the reception was not always good, and often made listening impossible. That has all changed with the internet. You can listen to radio stations in any language on the internet. (I mentioned this in chapter 8.) You can pick up good quality reception from any part of the world—sometimes in stereo. I have listened to broadcasts in a number of languages that I am learning.

Usually you will be able to find a link to the program guide on a station's home page so you can select the program you listen to.

The usefulness of these radio programs depends on the subject of the program and how much you understand. If you understand fairly well what is being said, it is possible to learn new words from the context in which they are used. If you understand very little, at least you get used to the sound of the language.

Audio files

You can conduct a search for audio files in your target language. If you can download an audio file with a transcript—especially on a subject that will be useful to you—then that is a great opportunity to reinforce your vocabulary in your chosen area. There are many such files available—you just have to look for them.

If you are interested in religious literature, you can download the Bible, the Koran and Buddhist and Hindu literature as both audio and text files. You can listen to, say, the Bible in Icelandic, while you read the Icelandic text and follow it in English as well.

Video files

I once downloaded a short one-minute training film in Malay from the Singapore Emergency Services website. I played it over and over until I understood what the presenters were saying. Short video clips are better in some ways than feature movies, because you are more likely to work your way right through them and translate the text. Various search engines such as WebCrawler and AltaVista allow you to search specifically for online video materials; for example, television news items in the language you are learning.

Shopping for language tools online

You can check out eBay and amazon.com to find items for sale that will help you learn your language. This can be useful when you are having trouble finding good courses and textbooks for the more exotic languages. The only problem is that you are buying the material sight unseen. At amazon.com you can read other people's reviews of the material, but that is not always a good or accurate guide. You need to use discrimination here—some people are looking for different things to you; some may want many drills and repetition, others feel that drills are a waste of time and want a different approach. I have often noted that some praise a book or program, giving it five stars for excellence, saying that it is exactly what they want, while others say the same book or program was useless for the exactly same reasons and give it one star. That is why you should always read *why* people like or don't like a book or course.

Despite the drawbacks, there is no harm in doing an amazon.com or eBay search for your target language and see what is on offer. You might decide to take the risk.

Language course websites

There are websites for many language courses on the internet, including Assimil, FSI, Living Language, Transparent Language and Pimsleur. They are worth a visit, particularly the Transparent Language site, which offers survival language courses that you can try at home, listen to and print out, as well as reading material in many languages and other resources, too. I would recommend their site whether you intend to buy Transparent Language material or not; it has much useful information. Audio Forum is another source of good and useful information about many languages.

Web addresses (URLs) for these sites are listed in appendix B (along with those of other useful sites). Check them out, but remember that they have an interest in selling you their material.

★ ★ ★

The internet has a wealth of information and material that will help you learn your target language. The resource is there, waiting for you to use it. Learning a language has never been so easy.

Advice for school and university students

nineteen
δεκαεννέα
dix-neuf
neunzehn
diecinueve
девятнадцать
sembilan belas
yhdeksäntoista

If you are a student studying a language you may not have chosen to learn, perhaps you are wondering how you can use the information in this book. Does it apply to you—especially if you are studying one of the so-called dead languages?

The answer is yes—there are certainly ways you can make your learning easier and more pleasant using the information you have read in earlier chapters.

Firstly, you should definitely find a recorded language program. Get used to listening to the language around your home or dormitory. Try to follow the learning plan outlined in chapter 10 as closely as you can.

Make sure you have at least one other textbook (beside your set course textbook) to learn from in parallel. It will explain the language structure differently, and will add also add variety.

You should read plenty of fun stuff in the language; buy comics, joke books and light reading material, or borrow them from the library. The problem with reading set texts is that you can grow to hate them. Read material of your own choice and make it enjoyable. When I suggest this, my students sometimes complain that I am adding to their workload. It is true. But I am making the workload much more pleasant. You will find this approach makes the load much easier to bear. Reading joke books and comics is quite different to reading your set textbook.

Visit social and cultural clubs and participate in activities if you can to surround yourself with the language and culture. Practise what you have learnt with the people you meet. Enjoy yourself.

Buy your own grammar book, so that you can read through a different or additional explanation of the grammar and language structures your teacher explains in class using the set text. Reading a different explanation can often give you new insight into what you have already learnt.

Use the internet. Print out pages from interesting websites you have found and use them for reading practice. Listen to online radio stations to get used to listening to the language.

Taking private lessons can be an excellent idea. Sometimes, just two or three lessons with the language explained from a different point of view can be very helpful. You don't need the lessons as much as people who are learning alone might, as you have your regular classes in which you can ask questions. However, if you have a question that you feel your teacher hasn't been able to explain to your satisfaction, an outside class is an opportunity to hear a different viewpoint.

Have your own total immersion days. You don't need many. You will find that even an occasional immersion day will give you a huge advantage over the other students.

Use the vocabulary methods described in chapter 9 to learn any words you keep forgetting. This will ensure you have them when you need them.

You will be restricted in the approach you take to learning grammar, but, as far as possible, use the two-wave method to master it. Race forward in your textbooks as fast as you can and worry about the grammar later. If you keep pushing ahead with the first wave, you will find you are likely to keep ahead of the rest of your class anyway. The grammar taught in the classroom will be familiar to you and you will find it much easier to grasp than the other students.

Make your own survival book. Learn the spoken language, even if you feel it is irrelevant to your course. If you are learning a language, you might as well learn to *use* it. It might be a good idea to put aside a set time for a practice session each day. Use the book and talk to yourself in the language.

Before an oral examination, spend time immersing yourself in the language. Speak to yourself in your target language right up to the time you walk into the examination room so you will be as fluent in the language as possible. This could make the difference between success and failure in your exam.

I remember reading a book by someone who had applied for a post in the British Foreign Service and had to sit an oral exam in a foreign language. Before he sat the exam he spent an hour or so visiting and chatting with speakers of the language, so that when he sat the examination, his mind was tuned to speak fluently. It must have worked, because he was accepted for his post.

Above all, treat the language course as a fun activity. Set out to enjoy it while your classmates are complaining and working at it.

Learning ancient languages

People have often asked me, 'Can I apply your methods to learning ancient languages?' and 'How can I practise speaking a language that is no longer in use?' It *is* possible to practise speaking 'dead' languages, and my methods can easily be adapted to this purpose.

A friend of mine was once asked to fill in for a lecturer in New Testament Greek at a theological college. He wasn't sure of his ability to teach the language, so he asked if I could help him, using my learning strategies. We came up with the idea of teaching the students the vocabulary from their textbook in record time. Although my friend was substituting, he invited me to give the lecture as a guest speaker. In a one-hour lesson, I taught the vocabulary from the first thirteen chapters of the college textbook. Some students who weren't even studying Greek sat in on this lecture and they memorised the vocabulary perfectly as well.

The strategies for learning a foreign vocabulary work equally well if the language is alive or dead, new or ancient. You can apply the method of making crazy pictures to any language you are learning. You will not only learn the words faster, you will enjoy it as well.

My general suggestions for learning an ancient language follow.

If a modern form of the language is spoken, learn this as well. For example, a student of New Testament Greek or Ancient Greek could learn Modern Greek as well. If you are learning Latin, learn Italian. If you are learning Biblical Hebrew, learn Modern Hebrew as well. This applies to any ancient language: even if your learning of the modern equivalent is only on a superficial level, it will help. I have heard lecturers argue against this. They say that students will be confused by the modern meanings of words, and that the modern pronunciation is different to the ancient. I am not convinced by their arguments.

Use the two-wave method for learning grammar as far as is possible. Push ahead with your textbooks so your reading is always ahead of your knowledge of grammar.

Have your total immersion days, or at least mini–immersion days. Put aside a few hours just to read and practise the language, to give your knowledge and understanding of the language a boost.

Make good use of any resources you can find on the internet. There is a lot of information out there about dead languages. The website I mentioned in chapter 18, <www.languages-on-the-web.com>, is full of useful links. It includes resources for ancient languages as well as contemporary spoken languages, so be sure to check it out. There are other websites devoted to individual languages that you can find by doing a search.

There is plenty of useful material out there—why not use it?

Language addicts

twenty
είκοσι
vingt
zwanzig
veinte
двадцать
dua puluh
kaksikymmentä

It may seem strange, and hard to believe, but there are people out there who are addicted to learning languages. When these people get together, they don't discuss learning a foreign language—they discuss the next ten languages they will learn.

I am definitely a language addict. I like to learn languages for their own sake. Offer me a good language course and I will take it. I just wish I had more time to indulge my interest or obsession. I remember remarking to the receptionist at the language school where I studied French that I envied her chance to learn as many languages as she wanted. (I had discovered that she listened to her Assimil language course through the day, and I thought she had a dream job—being able to study any of the languages available with the Assimil system.) She looked at me strangely. She wasn't an addict—she just wanted to learn Spanish and took the opportunity with the material at hand.

The smallest thing can trigger my interest in a language. On one occasion, I was travelling by train and found an Icelandic newspaper on the seat that someone had left behind. That was a treasure for me. I read it through from front to back and was pleasantly surprised at how much I was able to understand, mainly because of my knowledge of German and a little Swedish. I have been fascinated by Iceland and everything Icelandic ever since. I am looking forward to my first visit there. Sometimes salespeople ask me what my favourite holiday destination would be. I always tell them Iceland. They think I am making fun of them and get angry, but I am simply telling them the truth. I definitely intend to learn some Icelandic before I go — I have already downloaded some Icelandic learning material from the internet and I have an introductory course in Icelandic.

On another occasion, I received a Hebrew course in the mail that I hadn't ordered — it was apparently sent by mistake. I decided to keep it, so I paid for it and began learning Hebrew. Later, a friend signed up for a course of Hebrew lessons, and then found he had another university course at the same time, so he asked me if I would like to take his Hebrew lessons in his place. I willingly took his course and learnt Hebrew with the added help of my home-study program.

I regularly participate in an online forum for language addicts. Many of the forum members love spy movies in which the hero speaks in several languages, because they get a high from being able to understand what he or she is saying. When they cannot understand, they are inspired to learn yet another language. They love to read thrillers for the same reason.

I am the same: I love the excitement that comes from understanding something written or said in a new language. When we lived in Europe, I thought it was exciting that I was in a different country, especially a country in communist Eastern Europe, where I was able to speak with people on the street.

A Russian military officer once offered to take my photograph outside the Alexander Platz railway station in East Berlin. I immediately agreed and this photo is now a prize possession. Another time, I photographed a group of Russian soldiers in East

Berlin and someone grabbed my camera and explained it was illegal to photograph the Russian military in East Berlin. Apparently they were not supposed to be there, although they were in plain view. I muttered my apology and said I had no idea. I didn't volunteer the information that I had already taken the photo and they let me go. That photo is another prized possession. I think perhaps I am naive: I had no fear speaking with the military in Eastern Europe.

My knowledge of Eastern European languages has also helped me to learn things I might never have been able to find out otherwise. I had an enjoyable conversation with the minister of a church in a small village in Czechoslovakia where some of my mother's family came from. Neither of us had a language in common but by use of some German, Russian and Polish we were able to converse. (My friends in Poland said that Czech is very similar to Polish but I never noticed much similarity.) I wanted to know about any surviving members of my mother's family and this man was able to explain to me that they had all died in the war or left the area.

There is a discussion topic at the forum website called 'Your First Language'. When members post comments here, they often sound as though they are discussing their first love. They have a special place in their hearts for the first foreign language they ever learnt.

Members also discuss various approaches to learning languages. Different people have different methods, and it seems that most will not change their method for anyone, yet they are always looking for that elusive method or course that will enable them to learn more easily and more quickly.

Why are they addicted? I believe it is because each language you learn is a new adventure. You are meeting an unfamiliar and maybe exotic culture; you are learning new ways to say things—not just new words but a whole new means of expression. Often, the words chosen to express ideas give insight as to how a culture or society thinks.

Somebody once argued that it is not possible really to appreciate and understand Shakespeare until you have read the Chinese translation, but if you are studying the classics or a religious text, to fully understand them, you *must* study them in the original language. Often, there are shades of meaning and nuances in the original text you will never get from a translation. Many language addicts would agree with this point of view and believe that this is a good reason to learn a foreign language.

People become addicted to learning languages for many reasons. Someone was asked why he had learnt so many languages. He said that once he had begun learning he had just been too lazy to stop!

How to make a comeback

twenty-one
εικοσι ένα
vingt et un
einundzwanzig
veintiuno
двадцать один
dua puluh satu
kaksikymmentäyksi

Learning a language does take effort and some willpower. Sometimes you have to work at keeping yourself motivated. Write down your own plan for learning the language and keeping yourself enthusiastic. If your plan doesn't work for you, vary it until it does. Offer yourself treats — bribe yourself to work at the language.

Still, it is inevitable that you will lapse in your study of a language at some time. The reasons might be out of your control: perhaps a family crisis or a frantic period at work. No matter what the reason, there is a procedure you can follow to make a comeback.

First of all, don't become discouraged. You don't plan for a lapse, but you don't let one defeat you, either. You are going to learn the language anyway. You re-evaluate your goals — what you want from the language — and you keep going.

I like to have an immersion day for my comeback or, at least, a mini–immersion day. However, don't put off your comeback while you wait for the chance to have an immersion day. Begin again now and have your immersion day later if necessary.

Firstly, go back about three to five chapters before the point in your textbook at which you stopped your study. Read these lessons through. If you are comfortable with them, continue. If not, go back another five chapters. You can do up to two or three times your usual amount each day while you are catching up. After two or three days, you will feel as though you had never stopped. Often when you revise your lessons, you will understand things you had missed completely before. On occasion, I have actually gone back to lesson one in my main textbook and read and worked my way through to the last lesson I completed. I not only feel re-motivated, I often find I understand the lessons better by looking at them afresh.

Look at the positives. You come back to the language with a fresh perspective. Do the things that you know from experience will motivate you. Treat yourself, too. Do all of your favourite things to tune your mind to the language again: visit a restaurant, read a comic book, listen to the music or watch a video.

Many who lapse do so permanently—they never take up their language study again. Determine now that you won't fall into that category. Set yourself some new language goals. Take a class. Visit a club or organisation where you can immerse yourself in the language. Read through this book again to motivate yourself. Begin again. Don't let your study go to waste.

Afterword

There is nothing like the thrill of speaking a new language, understanding and being understood.

I have a good friend in Australia who is Dutch. His brother came to visit from the Netherlands and I was invited over to meet him. We spent an enjoyable evening together speaking Dutch. That was my most intensive Dutch language lesson ever. I had only played at the language before, but I surprised myself with my fluency. Sometimes you simply have to jump in at the deep end before you realise how much of a language you do understand.

Maybe you don't consider yourself an enthusiast at all. Perhaps you are learning a language because you feel you have to, and you have read this book only because you wanted to achieve your goal using the easiest and least painful method possible. Even if this is so, you will still feel pleasure in communicating with other people in your new language. I guarantee it.

Being willing to try to communicate in another language creates opportunities for all sorts of interesting encounters. I was travelling in Poland with my family when a police officer stopped us for a routine check. He wanted to look at our car and the things we had brought with us from the west. (Our friends in Poland told us that this was common.) He only spoke Polish. I told him I didn't speak Polish but he wouldn't accept that. He insisted I speak and answer his questions in Polish. To my surprise, I discovered that I was able to do so. With the Polish I knew and the help of the forms we had filled at the border, I was able to understand and answer all of his questions. The questions were basic and my answers were very simple, but I was able to explain that we were visiting Poland because my mother's family had originally come from Poland to Australia about one hundred and fifty years before. We wanted to see where they had come from.

Speaking other languages can also be great for your ego. I was once in our local newsagent's store when another customer wanted to buy something but had no idea how to ask for it in English.

I was able to ask her, '*Parlez-vous français?*' No.

'*Sprechen Sie Deutsch?*' No.

'*Gavaritye vy po russki?*' No.

'*Czy pani mówi po polsku?*' No.

'*¿Habla Ud. español?*' No.

'*Parla italiano?*' No.

Eventually I found out that she spoke Maltese. With a little encouragement, she was able to let me know she wanted a hard cover and binder for her street directory. They had one, she bought it, and everyone was happy. The people in the newsagents had known me for years but didn't know I spoke multiple languages. They were impressed. Knowledge of many languages is commonplace and taken for granted in many parts of the world, but it is not expected in Australia.

You will experience pride as your proficiency in your new language grows. I remember being pleased when someone in Germany asked me which part of Germany I came from. They couldn't quite place my accent. They thought my accent was due to the fact that I spoke a German dialect. It made my day.

We lived for three years in a small village in Bavaria, which did in fact have its own dialect. When people from my parent company in Hanover in the north of Germany came to visit, I had to interpret because they couldn't understand a word the locals were saying. The dialect was unintelligible outside the immediate area. If you travelled to a town ten kilometres away they spoke an entirely different dialect (which was much easier to understand). So, here I was, a foreigner, helping Germans understand and speak with other Germans.

Apart from satisfying your ego, knowledge of at least one other language will give you an appreciation for other people and how they think. Often understanding a language will give you insights into the thought processes of the people who speak it. You can read their literature in the original. Often subtitles for a movie or an interview on television will leave out the subtle nuances of what the speakers are saying. When you understand the language you will appreciate and understand more of what is actually being said.

More than anything else, though, learning a language is fun. A very good friend of mine in Germany is a professional interpreter. He is German and generally translates from English to German. We were in Munich and I was asked to speak to a group of people about some of my experiences. More than half of the listeners were American so I spoke in English and he interpreted for German members of the audience. When I was part way through my presentation he gave a translation I wasn't happy with so I repeated what I had said in German, so he translated back into English. I continued on, speaking in German, and he continued translating to English. Everyone thought it was funny, because neither of us was speaking his native language. And it was fun. We both enjoyed ourselves.

Learning a language is an adventure. Travelling in a foreign country is much more enjoyable and exciting when you speak the language — even if you only speak it poorly. You can have your own language experiences and stories to tell the folks back home.

I hope this book has inspired you to learn a language and enrich your life. I wish you success as you begin your language adventure.

I would like to invite you to visit my website. You will find it at <www.speedmathematics.com>. I regularly post interesting and useful information there for language learners. There are links to language websites and ideas and helpful resources for general language study. Visit it from time to time to see what is new.

Appendix A
Model survival course

In chapter 5, we talked about making your own survival course. In this appendix you will find basic model phrases, sentences and conversations. You can photocopy this appendix for your own private use and fill in the spaces provided to create your own survival booklet. (The first blank line is for your target language translation and the second line is for the literal English translation.)

Alternatively, if the material included here does not meet your specific needs, use it to develop your own booklet, adapting it to suit your purposes.

I recommend breaking your survival language book into sections of around ten to twenty sentences, so that they will be easy to revise. Try to make the breaks between sections natural, so that each contains one or two complete conversations.

You will notice that some phrases and sentences, such as 'thank you' and 'What is your name?' are repeated in more than one conversation or scenario. This is deliberate—these are in fact high-frequency expressions you will need again and again, in many different situations. I feel it is important to use words and expressions you are learning in context like this—it makes them easier to remember.

I have also given several sentences which say the same thing in various ways. This allows you to learn and become comfortable with several different structures which can be adapted to fit any situation.

If you create your own booklet, I would recommend using this sort of repetition—it really helps you to build your skills quickly.

Once you have finished work on your booklet, the next step is to make a recording of it. If you can, ask a native-speaker friend to read the text aloud into a tape recorder. If you can't find a native speaker, you can always record yourself reading the text. Just do the best you can. Record the foreign text only—don't include the English translation on the tape. Play the tape every day. The phrases will soon become part of your working knowledge of the language, with very little effort on your part. This is a great start to learning the language. The phrases and vocabulary you will learn are important in day-to-day situations, but they will also help you with further language study. They provide a foundation you can build on.

Even if you are only going on a short holiday, being able to communicate at a basic level will make an enormous difference to your experience of a country and its people. I guarantee that you will get good use out of your survival course book.

English	Target language
Good day.	....
	....
Good morning.	....
	....
Good afternoon.	....
	....
Good evening.	....
	....
Good night.	....
	....
Good bye.	....
	....
Yes.	....
	....
No.	....
	....
Please.	....
	....

Thank you.

You're welcome.

Excuse me.

I am sorry.

What is your name?

My name is …

What is your nationality?

I am Australian/American/British/
Canadian/a New Zealander.

What is your address?

....

....

My address is ...

....

....

Where is your baggage?

....

....

Here is my baggage.

....

....

Please open your
case/suitcase/handbag.

....

....

Please open this case.

....

....

Please follow me.

....

....

Please come with me.

....

....

How long will you be staying?

....

....

Where will you be staying? ....

....

What is the purpose of your visit? ....

....

I am here on business. ....

....

I am here to attend a conference. ....

....

I am a student/tourist. ....

....

Do you have anything to declare? ....

....

No, nothing. ....

....

May I see your passport? ....

....

Where is your passport?

....

....

Here is my passport.

....

....

What is this/that?

....

....

Do you speak English?

....

....

I speak a little.

....

....

I understand a little English.

....

....

I understand if you speak slowly.

....

....

Please say it slowly.

....

....

Please speak slowly.

....

....

Fast Easy Way to Learn a Language

Can you please repeat that?

....

....

Please write it down.

....

....

I am sorry, I don't understand.

....

....

I would like to change some money.

....

....

I want to change $100.

....

....

How much will I get for $1000?

....

....

Please call a taxi.

....

....

Where can I find a taxi?

....

....

Can you please take me
to this address?

....

....

Do you know where it is?

....

....

How much will it cost?

....

....

Is it far?

....

....

No, it is near.

....

....

Please keep the change.

....

....

Thank you very much.

....

....

You're welcome.

....

....

Where is the toilet?

....

....

Where is the women's/men's toilet?

....

....

I would like to use the toilet.

....

....

I need to use the toilet.

....

....

I would like to wash.

....

....

I need to wash my hands.

....

....

The toilets are upstairs/downstairs.

....

....

Where are the stairs?

....

....

The stairs are on your right/left.

....

....

The stairs are in front of you.

....

....

Where is the lift (elevator)?

....

....

The lift is behind you.

....

....

Here is the escalator.

....

....

The escalator is over there.

....

....

I am tired.

....

....

I want to go to my room now.

....

....

I need to sleep.

....

....

I have reserved a room.

....

....

What is your name?

....

....

My name is …

....

....

Do you have a single/double room?

....

....

Do you have a room
with a bath/shower?

....

....

We have a single room.

....

....

Does it have a telephone?

....

....

Here is your key.

....

....

Please fill in this form.

....

....

Please sign here.

....

....

Where is my room?

....

....

Your room is upstairs/downstairs.

....

....

Your room is on the ground floor/
first floor/second floor.

....

....

Can I have something to eat now?

....

....

We would like to eat now.

....

....

Do you have room service?

....

....

Fast Easy Way to Learn a Language

Can I order breakfast/lunch/dinner?

....

....

I would like to eat in my room.

....

....

Where is the restaurant?

....

....

Please sit down/be seated.

....

....

May I see the menu?

....

....

Certainly, madam/sir.

....

....

What is this/that?

....

....

I would like a cup of tea/coffee.

....

....

Do you want a cup of coffee with milk?

....

....

I would like a cup of coffee
with cream, please.

....

....

I would like a cup
of black coffee, please.

....

....

Do you want red or white wine?

....

....

I would like a glass of red wine, please.

....

....

Would you like to eat now?

....

....

Can I order something to eat?

....

....

I would like some soup.

....

....

What is the soup of the day?

....

....

I would like some bread.

....

....

Can I have some more butter, please?

....

....

May I have a glass of water, please?

....

....

Would you like some chicken?

....

....

I would like a beefsteak.

....

....

Would you like it rare,
medium or well-done?

....

....

I would like it well-done, please.

....

....

Enjoy your meal!

....

....

Would you like dessert?

....

....

Can I have some ice-cream, please? ....

....

May I have the bill, please? ....

....

Thank you very much. ....

....

You're welcome. ....

....

Do you have a map of the city? ....

....

Where is a telephone? ....

....

Where is the post office? ....

....

Do you know where I can find
an internet cafe? ....

....

Where is a bank?

....

....

Where can I find an ATM?

....

....

Where is the railway station?

....

....

Go left/right/straight ahead.

....

....

Take the first/second/
third street on the left/right.

....

....

Where is the airport?

....

....

How far is it to the airport?

....

....

How long will it take to get there?

....

....

Is there an airport bus?

....

....

Where is the bus stop?

....

....

I don't know.

....

....

Could I have a ticket to ..., please?

....

....

Could I have a one-way ticket, please?

....

....

Could I have a return ticket, please?

....

....

Is this seat free?

....

....

Certainly.

....

....

No, it is taken.

....

....

Can I help you?

....

....

Do you want something?

....

....

What are you looking for?

....

....

Do you sell toys?

....

....

I would like to buy an umbrella.

....

....

I need a belt.

....

....

No, I don't need a belt.

....

....

How much is this?

....

....

It is $40.

....

....

It is very expensive.

....

....

It is too expensive.

....

....

I need a pen.

....

....

I would like a blue/black/red pen.

....

....

I need some new shoes.

....

....

Do you have a cheap
dictionary, please?

....

....

Here is a good, cheap dictionary.

....

....

It is too big/small.

....

....

I need a small dictionary.

....

....

I would like this one/that one, please.

How is the weather today?

It is fine/cloudy/rainy.

It is not raining now.

It may rain tomorrow.

If it is fine, we can go to the park.

If it rains tomorrow, I think
I will stay at the hotel and work.

You can work at the office.

What would you like to do today?

....

....

Would you like to see a movie?

....

....

No, I would like to buy some souvenirs.

....

....

Where can I find a souvenir shop?

....

....

_____

Good day. Can I help you?

....

....

I would like to see Mr Smith.

....

....

I have an appointment with Mr Smith.

....

....

Is Mr Smith here?

....

....

I will see if he is free.

....

....

He is here.

....

....

He will be with you shortly.

....

....

May I see Mrs/Miss/Ms Brown?

....

....

She is not here.

....

....

She is in Sydney.

....

....

Here is my telephone number.

....

....

Here is my card.

....

....

Come in, please.

....

....

Please take a seat.

....

....

What is your name?

....

....

My name is …

....

....

What is your surname (family name)?

....

....

My surname is …

....

....

How do you spell that?

....

....

Could you spell that, please?

....

....

It is spelt …

....

....

Please write it down.

....

....

Where do you live?

....

....

I live in/at ...

....

....

What is your nationality?

....

....

I am Australian/American/British/
Canadian/a New Zealander.

....

....

I am from Australia/New Zealand.

....

....

What is your address?

....

....

What is your telephone number?

....

....

May I have your address
and telephone number?

....

....

How are you?

....

....

Very well, thank you. And you?

....

....

Please meet my wife/husband/
daughter/son.

....

....

This is my mother/father/
sister/brother.

....

....

I am pleased to meet you.

....

....

Would you like something to drink?

....

....

Yes, please.

....

....

No, thank you.

....

....

Please help yourself.

....

....

Fast Easy Way to Learn a Language

Thank you.

....

....

You're welcome.

....

....

How long have you been here?

....

....

I arrived yesterday.

....

....

We came here last week/a month ago.

....

....

When do you leave?

....

....

I leave tomorrow.

....

....

We are leaving in a week/in a month.

....

....

_____

I don't feel well.

....

....

I have a headache.

....

....

Do you want anything?

....

....

Do you need me?

....

....

Would you like an aspirin?

....

....

No, I am fine, thank you.

....

....

I would like a headache tablet.

....

....

Do you have any aspirin?

....

....

Can I have a glass of water?

....

....

I want to go to my hotel.

....

....

I need to sleep.

I think I have a fever.

Are you hot/cold?

Where is the chemist/
pharmacy/drugstore?

I think I need a doctor.

I need to see a doctor immediately.

Please call a doctor.

Please call an ambulance.

Where is the hospital?

Please speak slowly.

....

....

Can you please repeat that?

....

....

_____

Help!

....

....

Look out!

....

....

Please call the police!

....

....

Please call the Australian/
British/Canadian/New Zealand/
United States embassy.

....

....

I would like to telephone my embassy.

....

....

Appendix B
Language websites

Websites listed in this appendix are included as a guide and for your information only. The addresses provided here are valid at the time of publication and I believe that most are likely to remain valid for some time.

Language resource websites

Here are some websites that offer resources and support for language learners. You might like to check them out to see what they offer. Some sites have sample lessons available for downloading so you can evaluate their methods before you buy.

Word2Word

The Word2Word site will help you find free internet language-learning material and useful links. A very good site!

<www.word2word.com/coursead.html>

Languages-on-the-web

The Languages-on-the-web site publishes dual-language stories and general links for learning many languages. An excellent site! This is an essential resource for anyone studying another language.

<www.languages-on-the-web.com>

How-to-learn-any-language.com forum

The How-to-learn-any-language forum is a great resource for anyone contemplating learning another language. It provides a forum for both novices and experts. Forum participants discuss methods, resources and problems connected with learning a language. You can get help from native speakers of your target language and ask for advice on any language topic. I love it.

<http://how-to-learn-any-language.com/forum>

Multilingual Books

The Multilingual Books site is a US-based online store at which you can buy general language materials.

<www.multilingualbooks.com>

200words-a-day.com

The 200 words a day website is worth visiting, especially if you are studying French, Spanish or German. It is a resource for learning vocabulary which uses a similar method to that taught in this book, and has humorous colour cartoons to help your memory.

<www.200words-a-day.com>

Language course websites

Linguaphone

Linguaphone is a pioneer of language teaching programs.

<www.linguaphone.co.uk>

Assimil

Assimil is a pioneer of language study programs in Europe.

<www.assimil.com>

Transparent Language

Transparent Language has some excellent cassette/CD and computer programs. It also offers free survival courses for some languages with audio.

<www.transparent.com>

Foreign Service Institute (FSI)

Many people swear by the Foreign Service Institute (FSI) programs. They are certainly worth checking to see what they offer. You can download some sample audio files to try them from the sites listed below.

<www.multilingualbooks.com/fsi.html>

<www.101language.com/fsi.html>

Audio Forum

Audio Forum offers full language programs in a wealth of languages. If you are learning one of the more obscure languages, this site might offer the best course available for your purpose.

<www.audioforum.com>

Pimsleur

Pimsleur has many devoted followers. The Pimsleur Direct site and the Sybervision free audio site both have sample files of Pimsleur language programs you can try for free on your own computer.

<www.pimsleur.com>

<www.sybervision.com/freeaudio.htm>

Berlitz

Berlitz has a huge range of language programs.

<www.berlitz.com>

Unforgettable Languages

Unforgettable Languages teaches the same method we have used in this book to memorise foreign vocabulary, and offers programs in many languages—probably including your target language. Try a free sample lesson on their website.

<www.unforgettablelanguages.com>

Living Language

Living Language has excellent programs—I have several myself.

<www.randomhouse.com/livinglanguage>

Nodtronics

The Nodtronics site offers CDs for seventy languages at a very affordable price. It includes many obscure languages you may have difficulty finding elsewhere. Nodtronics offers the Transparent Language programs in Australia and New Zealand.

<www.nodtronics.com.au/products/education_language/index.html>

Language-specific sites

UK India — Urdu, Hindi, Arabic and related languages

If you are learning an Indian language like Urdu or Hindi, or you would like to learn Arabic or Hebrew, then try UK India's website. It has material you can download so that you can use it when you are not connected to the internet.

<www.ukindia.com>

Synergy Spanish

Synergy Spanish is an excellent site for downloading Spanish lessons. The speaker guides you through the lessons in English, which I don't normally like or recommend, but they are so good that I make an exception. The lessons last around five minutes, so it is not so difficult or time-consuming to review past lessons.

<www.synergyspanish.com>

Platiquemos — Spanish

Like Synergy, Platiquemos has an excellent site and offers a program for learning Spanish. You can download sample lessons to try.

<www.platiquemos-letstalk.com>

Golosa — Russian

For Russian I recommend a visit to Golosa. This site offers text, audio and video files to help you learn and improve your Russian.

<www.gwu.edu/~slavic/golosa>

Learn Greek Online

For learning Greek, Learn Greek Online is an excellent site.

<www.kypros.org/LearnGreek>

Focus on Malaysia

You can find a complete course in Malay at this website.

<http://pgoh.free.fr/Malay_Language>

A Japanese guide to Japanese grammar

An excellent guide to basic Japanese grammar is available to download free from this site.

<www.guidetojapanese.org>

On-line Chinese Tools

On-line Chinese Tools is a great site offering resources for students learning Chinese.

<www.mandarintools.com>

Other online resources

Other resources you will find on the web include online dictionaries and web translation services.

Online dictionaries — Freelang.net

I mentioned Freelang.net in the discussion of online dictionaries in chapter 18. This site is a great resource for language enthusiasts: it has dictionaries for seventy-nine languages you can download to your computer for free.

<www.freelang.net>

Web translation sites

For translating materials in foreign languages, I recommend both AltaVista's Babel Fish and Google's translation service. If using Google, select 'Language Tools' on the Google home page. Refer back to chapter 18 for further details.

<http://babelfish.altavista.com>

<www.google.com>

The author's website

Please visit my website, Learning Unlimited Australia. New information about languages and language learning is uploaded frequently.

<www.speedmathematics.com>

Index